TO

BE A

CHER:

AN

TION

TO

TION

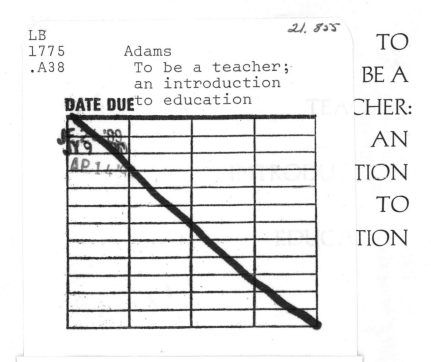

Sam Adams

John L. Garrett, Jr.

Louisiana State University

TO BE A TEACHER: AN INTRODUCTION TO EDUCATION

PRENTICE-HALL, INC., ENGLEWOOD CLIFFS, NEW JERSEY

13-922906-X

Library of Congress Catalog Card Number: 69-17485
Printed in the United States of America

Current printing (last digit):

10 9 8 7 6 5 4 3 2

PRENTICE-HALL INTERNATIONAL, INC., *London*
PRENTICE-HALL OF AUSTRALIA, PTY. LTD., *Sydney*
PRENTICE-HALL OF CANADA, LTD., *Toronto*
PRENTICE-HALL OF INDIA PRIVATE. LTD., *New Delhi*
PRENTICE-HALL OF JAPAN, INC., *Tokyo*

PREFACE

We feel that many people who take the introductory course in education could be described as interested in but not totally committed to a career in teaching. Any major career decision of this nature should be based upon information about the field of interest. We attempted in this book to provide such information, but have made no attempt to cover the entire broad field of education. Rather, we have tried to concentrate on the type of material which, in our opinion, would be of assistance to a student as he seeks to answer the vital question: Shall I be a teacher?

We suggest to teachers who use this book in teaching that they view it as a textbook—but not as a course. We feel that educational information of a local nature is very important to students, since many teachers show a strong preference for teaching in their own communities. Hence we suggest that in the introductory education course, the teacher draw extensively from local and state sources. We feel that such a procedure helps to localize—and to some degree personalize—the course.

We have tried to raise questions in the body of the text and in the "Questions and Activities" at the end of each chapter that will assist in this undertaking.

SAM ADAMS
JOHN L. GARRETT, JR.

CONTENTS

II
TEACHING

I

TEACHERS

Presumably you have an interest in the field of teaching; otherwise you would not be using this textbook. However, you cannot be sure that teaching is your field until you are well-informed about it. A basic assumption in this book is that you are interested in and at least partially committed to the teaching profession. A prime goal of the authors is to assist you in learning more about teachers and teaching, that you may make your career choice wisely.

You will note that this book is organized around two central topics—teachers and teaching. Probably this could have been made to sound more impressive by using other terms. But we are especially eager for you to get a clear picture of the educational enterprise in terms of people and processes—that is, teachers and teaching.

In your own educational career, who was your best teacher? Most people have little difficulty in selecting those who were truly exceptional. Having made your selection, try to think for a moment just why he was outstanding. This may be a bit more difficult. But very likely your list of characteristics can be summarized in a few terms such as "he was a warm human being," "he tried to be help-ful," "he was very effective," and nearly always your list would include "he was fair."

Perhaps it is a platitude, but teachers are people—very impor-tant people. Hence this section is devoted to the people of teaching.

1

WHAT IS A TEACHER?

In one of Thomas Wolfe's books, there is an account of the political figure who was trying to define "the people." After several false starts, he sputtered that, "The people are *the people*." This is frequently the result when we try to define "a teacher" —"A teacher is *a teacher!*"

Yet each of us has his own concept of the teacher. Such a concept is almost inevitably based upon individual experience. Try to think of a teacher in the abstract and almost invariably you will find yourself thinking of individual teachers you have known. Most people think of a teacher as the person who assumes the leadership role in the teaching-learning process. This encompasses widely diverse teaching situations, both formal and informal.

IT IS HARD TO DESCRIBE A TEACHER

Imagine for a moment that we had an educational system that was national in scope and operation. Imagine that all teachers were required to operate within prescribed guidelines. In short, imagine that some central *authority* required that all teachers do the same things and in the same way. Even then, can you think of ways in which the teachers in one community would differ from those in another?

The teacher's role changes

In American society, there is no such thing as a static profession. The role of the modern-day doctor, for example, is far different from that of his predecessor of a century ago. The same is true of the lawyer and of others. Certainly, the role of the teacher in modern society is far removed from that of earlier teachers. Further, there is no reason to assume that present-day concepts will apply in future decades.

Not only does change in the teacher's role become apparent when viewed in the historic sense, but it is also seen as we shift from one community to another. Certain practices of teachers in one community might be looked upon with disfavor in another. A case in point might be that of teachers holding public office. In some areas this is common practice; others have a specific policy against such activities.

Historical Concept of the Teacher. American educational literature is replete with references to the one-room school. It is easy for us to overlook the fact that this was also a one-*teacher* school. This meant, of course, that this teacher taught all students of all levels in all subject areas. Can you imagine a more impossible task? Another feature, sometimes overlooked, is that grouping students into grade levels is a fairly recent development. Hence, for many years the teacher in the one-room school tried to teach his students individually. Obviously, this teacher was faced with continuous frustration and failure if for no other reason than that he was trying to deal with a hopeless task. We can feel grateful that the role of the teacher has changed a great deal in this regard.

Another historical concept of the teacher was that of the stern disciplinarian. Indeed, many communities judged the success or failure of their teacher-of-the-moment on the degree to which he could "dis-cip'-line" the school. Someone has estimated that a student in an ungraded one-room school might have had as little as twenty minutes per day of actual instruction. The remainder of the very long day (8:00 a.m. to 5:00 p.m. continuously), he was simply "in storage." Under such circumstances endless behavioral problems were to be expected. Consequently, the teacher of the period in question was seldom out of reach of a board, switch, or leather strap. The role of the teacher in this area has changed drastically as we have learned more about pupil behavior. However, some teachers will still find the area of discipline to be a troublesome one.

During the earlier decades of American educational history, the teacher was frequently an itinerant, with practically no community ties. Short school terms and low salaries served to make it impractical for many teachers to establish a home in the area of employment. Consequently, the teachers who had families often lived apart from the families during the school term. This situation was further complicated by the fact that job security was practically nonexistent. Many teachers taught a single term, then moved on to other positions. The result was that teachers were seldom accepted within a community in the sense that settled residents were accepted. Hence, not only was the *role* of the teacher changing; the teachers themselves were constantly changing.

Teacher Concept as Observed in Some Small Schools. Just as the function of the teacher changes from decade to decade, it also changes from community to community.

Let us assume a situation in which a teacher is working in a small school, located in a rural area. In the first place, he would probably know and be known by all of the students in the school. This frequently gives rise to counseling situations outside of class. Further, the teacher in such a school is very likely to be on an extensive, as compared to an intensive, assignment. High school teachers might teach classes in two, three, or even four areas. The elementary teacher would commonly have more than a single grade represented in his classroom. Furthermore, certain administrative and housekeeping chores would frequently have to be assigned to faculty members in schools too small to employ specialized personnel for such work.

The role of the teacher in the community is of considerable importance in rural areas. In the first place, people usually know each other, and they expect to get to know the teachers. It is assumed in many such situations that the teachers will be interested—and active—in community affairs. Because the teachers are usually among the best-educated citizens of the town or village, it is sometimes assumed that the teachers will function as community leaders.

Hence you can see that a teacher employed in the type of situation just described would need to be versatile and willing to work. An outgoing type of personality is most helpful, and the self-confidence required to move into unfamiliar situations can make a tremendous contribution to the teacher's effectiveness in this type of situation. Have you ever lived in a rural community? If so, what was the role of the teachers?

Teacher Concept in Some Large Schools. Going to the other extreme, let us consider the role of the teacher in a large school. Under these conditions, a high school teacher would likely teach in a single subject area and might well teach multiple sections of a single course. Hence, fairly intensive specialization is common practice. In view of the large number of students, teachers frequently know only those students with whom they come in direct contact. Also, only to a minimal extent are these teachers usually involved in "extras," such as clerical chores. Some teachers who make the transition from smaller schools to large schools frequently find, with a sense of frustration, that they are practically unknown to students and even to colleagues outside their own spheres of operation.

To a considerable degree, the points mentioned above are applicable to the teacher in the community. Only the exceptional urban teacher has extensive contact with parents of his own students. Leadership roles in nonschool activities are uncommon. In short, the teacher in a large urban school is likely to be simply another member of the community, with no *ex officio* duties of the type so common in smaller schools.

Many functions of the teacher are somewhat abstract

Contributing to the difficulty of defining "a teacher" is the fact that we have difficulty in defining the task of the teacher. There can be little doubt as to the ultimate goal of a farmer, an electrician, or a file clerk. Indeed, a vast number of employment areas adapt themselves to precise and detailed job descriptions. Is this true of the teacher? When can a teacher say that his task is completed? Or when can he be *sure* that he has done a good job? What is your own concept of the work of a teacher?

The Act of Instruction is Hard to Describe. Certainly we would agree that the prime task of the teacher is to teach. But this constitutes an oversimplification, since it gets us back to the basic difficulty described earlier. It is not uncommon to find two teachers in the same school, both considered to be very effective instructors, who go about their work in entirely different ways. One might be quite formal while the other is informal. One might depend primarily on class discussion while the other makes extensive use of class projects. Further, if each of these teachers were required to use the technique of the other, it is likely that the results would be unsatisfactory to all concerned.

It has long been recognized that there are many instructional procedures available to teachers. However, out of these there has never emerged a pattern which could be described as *the* method. Consequently, the act of instruction itself has never been described in terms of wide applicability.

Promotion of Individual Growth is an Abstract Goal. The modern American school has long since set for itself far more complex tasks than that of imparting information. For example, as an institution designed to serve "all the children of all the people," the school is expected to promote the personal as well as the educational growth of each student. Possibly this may sound relatively simple.

Again, the goal in question is somewhat abstract because there is no fixed method or procedure that applies. Consider Tommy, a first grader who has grown up under the wing of an overly protective mother. He has never had to make decisions for himself, he cries frequently, he is lost in trying to cope with a problem. On the other hand, there is Billy, also a first grader. He is one of a large family in which the parents have encouraged each member to "stand on his own two feet." Making his own decisions is no problem to him. However, he is so much of an individualist that he has trouble working in a group situation. What are some steps the teacher would need to take in promoting the individual growth of Tommy? Of Billy? To what degree are the two lists similar? Dissimilar?

The complexity of the teacher's task is even clearer when we add to the list Mary, Sally, Jimmy, and approximately 25 other first graders in a particular classroom. Yet the teacher's goal is to promote the growth of *each* of these individuals.

Then There Is "Development of Wholesome Attitudes." Obviously this is an objective of major importance. One's general outlook on life is influenced by school experiences. Yet what would be more difficult than reducing to a step-by-step procedure the teacher's method of working toward this goal?

If a particular student is academically weak, by the time he reaches the junior high level, he has come to accept defeat as his inevitable lot in academic tasks. This defeatist attitude may well carry over into all his activities, so that he makes no particular effort to succeed. The teacher is directly involved in trying to develop a more positive outlook on the part of this student. Yet the procedure—and indeed, the task—is basically abstract in that it cannot be categorized.

In recent years we have learned a great deal about the promotion of mental health among school children. This, of course, is directly related to the promotion of wholesome attitudes. As is true of many teacher functions, there is little room here for a "give them all the same treatment" approach. A method that would help one student might well aggravate the problems of another. The _teacher's role in the development of wholesome attitudes_ on the part of her students is of vital importance and a major responsibility that he must assume. Yet it is a role that is quite difficult to define.

There Are Many Others. Over the years, several groups of distinguished educators have attempted to describe the basic function of American education. The work of some of these groups is described elsewhere in this book. The lists of goals growing out of such studies have been helpful. However, many of the objectives, obviously important, are very difficult to implement. Consider, for example, "ethical character" or "worthy home membership." Who would question their importance? But how would *you* go about promoting ethical character in your own class?

Suppose you had a job packing cans of tomatoes in crates. You would have no doubt when the crate was filled to capacity —which would mark the "success point" in your relatively simple task. You could easily define your job in terms of what you were supposed to do, how you were supposed to do it, and when the task was completed. Compare this with the task of the teacher. In what ways do the two jobs differ?

Another reason for the difficulty we encounter in trying to define "a teacher" is the abstract nature of many of the goals toward which he is working.

Teachers' concepts of their work differ

If you were to ask a random sample of Americans to describe the work of an electrician, many responses would be based upon "the most recent service I have asked an electrician to perform." You are doubtless familiar with the fable of the blind men and the elephant. Each "saw" the elephant in terms of his own personal experience.

However, wouldn't you expect an electrician to be able to describe his own work? Even this approach would not be effective among teachers, since each teacher has his own unique concept of his role and his task.

Some See Themselves as Subject-matter Specialists. Consider the case of the Spanish teacher who, in describing his position, puts a great deal of emphasis on the *Spanish* and slurs over the *teacher*. This might indicate that he prefers to identify with the subject area rather than with the profession. Indeed, many teachers, especially at the secondary level, seem to think of themselves as linguists, mathematicians, or scientists first and assign the teaching role a secondary position. This line of thinking is even more pronounced in higher education.

Do you see the attitude described above as being objectionable? A person has every right to be proud of his teaching field and to build up his subject-matter competence in that area. However, as a matter of being realistic, the work of a scientist *is* basically different from that of a science teacher.

There is little opportunity for an elementary teacher to see himself as a subject-matter specialist, since he works in many areas. However, one occasionally encounters an elementary teacher who will confide that, although he teaches in many subjects, his chief interest is in social studies, language arts, or some other specialty. Certainly we would not expect an elementary teacher to be equally interested in all areas. If he can follow up special interests by developing unusual proficiency in some areas without reducing his effectiveness in others, he is to be commended.

Some Teachers See Themselves as Child Development Specialists. There are some teachers who see their role as being almost totally child-centered. These teachers frequently take the position that content is quite incidental, and that the teacher simply provides an appropriate setting for growth.

This point of view is more likely to be found among elementary teachers than among secondary teachers. However, there are some secondary teachers, particularly those who work with adolescent groups, who become so involved with promoting personal and social growth that they lose sight of the importance of subject content.

You will note that the self-image of the teachers described above is in direct contrast to that described earlier—the subject-matter specialist. What do you see as an effective compromise between the two extremes as applied to your own teaching interest?

Can These Extreme Views Be Reconciled? Certainly they can

—and they are reconciled in the work of a vast majority of America's teachers. At the risk of oversimplification, let us think of the first group as representing the "I teach subject-matter" point of view. The second would represent the "I teach students" approach. Most teachers simply take the intermediate position of "I teach subject-matter to students."

Obviously there are many variations in emphases in the broad spectrum between the all-content and the child-centered extremes. However, the three positions described above illustrate the fact that there is no agreement among teachers concerning their basic role in society.

Teaching: Gateway to Other Lines of Work. Some teachers from the very first consider themselves to be teachers-in-transit. These are the people who, for reasons of their own, need to work for a while before they enter professional schools, business, or matrimony. Some distinguished figures in American history, including several presidents, are included in this group. Many of the teachers-in-transit have been quite effective as teachers. However, too many of them never really identify with teaching, since their attention is constantly fixed upon noneducational goals.

Teaching: A Source of Income. Is it inconsistent to mention money as a motive for teaching, in view of the generally low level of teacher salaries? A point that can be overlooked in this regard is that national averages tell only part of the story. In many communities, teachers belong to the higher-income group. Also, it is not uncommon for a husband to work in a different field while his wife teaches. When one compares their joint income with that of the husband only, he can see that the added income from teaching can make a great deal of difference. It would be closer to our ideal if we could say *nobody* in the profession sees teaching primarily as a source of income. However, when we view it realistically, we have to accept that some teachers are chiefly motivated by the salaries they receive.

In this section, we have touched upon five ways in which teachers view their work. The list could be continued almost indefinitely. However, this list is sufficiently extensive to illustrate a basic point: A major difficulty in defining "a teacher" is that there is no agreement, even among teachers themselves, as to his true function.

There are literally thousands of occupations open to American youth. The people in some of these occupations work primarily with machines. Others work with hand tools. Others work with materials. In the broader sense, teachers work with people. Certainly it would be an oversimplification to say that "a teacher is someone who works with people," since many nonteachers also work with people. But one of the prime characteristics of the teacher is that he is in almost continuous contact with people. Some of the ways in which teachers work with people are described below.

The teacher promotes pupil progress

In a general sense, the teacher is dedicated to the task of helping each pupil develop his own potential. Would it be defensible to say that the teacher helps each pupil grow? We know that physical growth would continue, with or without a teacher. However, if we view "pupil growth" in its broadest sense, then it is definitely an area of interest to the teacher.

Growth in Knowledge. As has been mentioned, the teacher in early America placed much emphasis on knowledge, or, as commonly applied, on memorization. Despite the broadened interpretation of the educative process, we still hold to the position that a student should *learn something*, that is, acquire knowledge. Let us illustrate this in mathematics. In the elementary school, the introduction of new concepts (sets, sentences, etc.) a few years ago was based upon an emphasis on understanding. Yet, regardless of how well a student might *understand* the process of multiplication, he still needs to *learn* the "multiplication tables." It should be emphasized that, in broadening the teacher's goals, we have not eliminated one of the most basic—helping the student acquire knowledge.

Pupil Self-concept. Another area in which the teacher hopes to promote pupil progress is in the matter of self-concept. Consider, for example, the extremely shy student. (Incidentally, he is to be found at all grade levels.) The alert teacher will look for ways to draw this student out. Another student might be lacking in self-confidence in a particular subject because of repeated failure. The teacher would try to give this youngster a taste of success in order to help him overcome his feelings of inadequacy. Other problems might include overaggressiveness, feelings of inferiority, and indifference. In each case, the teacher is interested in the pupil, his problem, and ways of helping him improve his self-concept.

Getting Along with Others. Only in fairly recent years have the schools felt any real obligation to help students in the matter of getting along together. However, who can doubt its importance? Have you ever known a person whose career suffered because he could not work with other people? Certainly other agencies, especially the home, are involved in helping a youngster overcome problems of this type. But the teacher can be a vital factor. Where would you find a more fitting laboratory in which one could "feel his way" toward better human relationships than in a classroom or on a school playground? This is an aspect of growth in which the teacher frequently operates in the background. He looks for ways to bring the student into group activities, then follows through to help as help is needed. The conscientious teacher is anxious to help his students learn the fine art of working together.

The Physical Aspects. The idea that the school should "educate the mind" has long since been expanded to include other activities. For example, in many parts of America, schools have helped educate entire communities in such matters as sanitation, dental hygiene, and others. The addition of physical and health education to elementary and secondary school curricula represented a major shift in emphasis. Even the school lunchroom, source of many student complaints, is frequently looked upon as a laboratory in nutrition.

The net result is that teachers now concern themselves with student progress in many aspects of growth other than the purely mental. Do you think this might account for the frequently quoted remark that we try to educate "the whole child?"

The teacher is a counselor

In his work with people, the teacher is frequently called upon to function in the role of counselor. Many schools, both elementary and secondary, have one or more counselors as members of the staff. Regardless of the effectiveness of these people, they cannot totally replace the classroom teacher as counselor.

In Academic Areas. If a high school student is in need of counsel because of difficulties in mathematics, it is very likely that he will turn to his mathematics teacher for such counsel. The same would hold for other subject areas, assuming that the teachers involved are of the type that students can approach. On many faculties, there will be teachers who have unique status with students—a type of status that would be difficult to define. Such teachers are often approached by students who are seeking academic counseling, even though the difficulty might be in a subject field far removed from that in which the teacher works. Of course, this teacher must use a great deal of discretion and must limit his operations to areas in which he is competent to counsel. In your own high school days, was there any one teacher who functioned in this capacity? Few teachers are totally inactive in academic counseling; their efforts supplement those of the professional staff in this regard.

In Vocational Matters. Again, the teacher can combine forces with the professional counselor in the matter of vocations. A modern-day student faces an amazingly complex array of vocational possibilities. The task of understanding the requirements of a proposed vocation, of appraising one's own potential, and of reconciling the two is a formidable one. Consequently, the student needs all the help he can get, including that of the teacher. The professional counselor works in a wide diversity of areas; hence his assistance might be somewhat generalized. However, when a would-be chemist comes down to such key questions as "Could I become a chemist?", he is very likely to turn to his chemistry teacher as a source of help.

In Personal Matters. Youngsters of all ages, and especially adolescents, occasionally need the counsel of an adult. In most cases, a parent cannot meet this need. As a result, many students will seek out a teacher with whom they can, in confidence, discuss their problems. Most experienced teachers, especially those in whose presence a student can be relaxed and comfortable, have functioned in this capacity. It is difficult to figure out how some students select their informal counselor. In one school, an older man whose teaching is primarily at the ninth grade level is unusually effective as confidant-counselor for high school girls.

The teacher works with colleagues

As a student in elementary and secondary schools, you were conscious of only a part of the work of the teacher—that part having to do with the teacher-pupil relationship. However, the teacher works with other people, too, and in a very important relationship. Included in the "other people" are faculty colleagues.

Informal Relationships. With the exception of the one-room schoolteacher, all teachers are in day-to-day contact with their fellow faculty members. Frequently, the degree of acceptance of a particular teacher is vitally influenced by this relationship. This acceptance, in turn, can affect the classroom performance of a teacher.

Imagine that you are teaching fourth grade in a large elementary school. The teacher in the adjoining room greets you each day with a scowl. His idea of a stimulating conversation is one in which he airs all of his complaints—physical, emotional, and professional. In the lounge, he speaks critically of any colleague who happens to be absent. Any assigned duty which is not clearly a part of his classroom work is looked upon as a special imposition. Do you think such a person could be truly effective as a teacher?

Obviously the above description does not apply to a large segment of teachers. Most teachers react in ways that are quite different from these. However, you do not need a very vivid imagination in order to picture the professional status of the teacher who, in the eyes of his colleagues, is permanently unhappy.

Formal Relationships. In addition to the informal relationships among faculty members described earlier, there are certain formally established patterns of cooperative work which are very important to the teacher. A case in point is faculty committees established within the school. For example, a teacher at the secondary level might be called upon to work with teachers who are in the same general subject area in the matter of adopting textbooks. Other tasks in which faculty committees frequently function include selecting tests to be used as part of a school testing program, reviewing grading and marking practices, reviewing registration and counseling procedures, and many others. To be truly effective, the teacher should be able to work with his colleagues in this kind of relationship.

Many of the local, state, regional, and national accrediting agencies require periodic self-studies on the part of school faculties. These self-studies are usually carried out through committee operations. For example, one faculty group might serve as a review committee for curriculum, another one for office procedures, another for faculty personnel, another for community relations, others for a great many additional studies. Obviously, the teacher who can maintain an effective working relationship with his colleagues is a very valuable member of the faculty during such operations as these.

Another way in which the teacher works with his colleagues is in what might be termed general faculty actions. It has come to be standard practice in many schools, both elementary and secondary, to have the faculty function as an informal type of legislative body. Parenthetically, it might be mentioned that some principals do not approve of this procedure and prefer to make the running of the school a one-man operation. However, those principals who depend upon faculty judgment or assistance in policy matters frequently get very good results from such methods. If a teacher is to have his voice heard and his judgment respected in general faculty actions of this type, obviously he must be a person who can work effectively with colleagues in other types of relationships.

The Teacher Works with the Administration. An important aspect of the teacher's work with people is the work with the administrative personnel of his school. Oddly enough some teachers who get along well with their students and with their colleagues find some difficulty in working with the administrators. For example, there are those who resent administrative direction of any sort. It is unfortunate but true that occasionally a teacher will place a stumbling block in the path of his own professional advancement because of difficulty in working with administrators.

The degree of administrative work expected of faculty members varies from school to school. However, there are certain types of such work that are pretty widely expected of teachers. Consider, for example, the matter of lunchroom duty. Many schools expect elementary teachers to stay with their classroom groups in the lunchroom and to serve as supervisors during this period. Also it is emphasized in many schools that there is a great deal of actual instruction that can be done best in the lunchroom. Another is playground duty. In many schools teachers are expected to supervise a group on the playground during play periods. Elementary teachers most commonly will supervise their own group. Secondary teachers might be expected to work with an assigned group of high school students. Another such duty is hall supervision during periods when large groups of people are unscheduled. Some teachers find these responsibilities to be somewhat unpleasant. On the other hand, they would doubtless agree that such tasks must be performed by someone.

Another way in which teachers frequently do administrative work involves money. In many schools teachers are expected to collect lunch money from a classroom or homeroom group. Certain special-assignment teachers such as the coach, band director, and speech teacher might find themselves dealing with considerable amounts of school funds as a result of collecting admission at various school functions. Homeroom teachers frequently handle fairly large amounts of money as a result of class fund-raising activities. It is important that the teacher handle these funds in a way that will be in keeping with administrative policies governing such matters.

One might occasionally find a teacher who insists that his sole responsibility is to his students. Such a teacher is, of course, failing to face up to the fact that there are other responsibilities that are inherent in his job. Any person who functions as a member of an organization is usually faced with such peripheral duties.

The teacher works with parents and community

It has been pointed out earlier that we have a great deal of variability from community to community in the teacher-community relationships. However, relationships of this type do exist in any school situation. Indeed, some teachers have to remind themselves occasionally that parents and the community make the school possible because necessary support comes from the community.

One type of parent relationship that is quite common is the parent conference. This can be especially difficult for a beginning teacher because of lack of confidence in his own ability to handle the situation. Many parents request a conference with a teacher simply because they want to know how they can function best in order to promote the intellectual growth of their sons and daughters. This is a wholesome thing and is to be encouraged. Certainly the best results on the part of the youngsters will be achieved when the school and the home work in a close relationship. Very frequently, the teacher can find the parents helpful allies in dealing with certain specific problems. In some cases, for example, potential disciplinary problems have been avoided because of parent-teacher conferences prior to the real emergence of the problem. It is a vital relationship and should be encouraged.

In the matter of community relationships, teachers find temselves involved in church and civic club activities. As has been mentioned earlier, in some communities a certain amount of this type of activity is expected of teachers. The modern-day teacher likes to think of himself as an integral part of the community in which he works. Consequently a reasonable amount of activity in church, civic, and community activities is probably desirable. Once again, the teacher who works most effectively with people will be the teacher to whom this type of relationship will be most satisfying.

A teacher many years ago described himself as being a "people engineer." While this might be a bit mechanical and might carry with it the implication of "people manipulation," there is a certain amount of truth in it. The work of the teacher involves materials, textbooks, classrooms, and many other items, but in the final analysis, the prime work of the teacher is the work that he does with people. Certainly it is true that the chief obligation is to the students. On the other hand, the effective teacher must be able to work with colleagues, with administrators, with parents, and with the community if he is to reach his full potential as a teacher.

When we think of a "profession" most of us immediately associate the term with law, medicine, and other lines of work of this type. A long-continuing debate has failed to settle the issue as to whether or not teaching is a profession. In essence, in some respects teaching has the characteristics of a profession and in certain others it does not. The term "teaching profession" comes up frequently in conversations and in professional meetings. This would indicate that many teachers identify themselves as professional people. You will note that we have not given a formal definition of the term "profession." What is your concept of the meaning of this term?

Specialized training is essential in teaching

Many authorities agree that a profession must be built upon the base of specialized training. It certainly is true that in this regard the teacher is a professional person, since he is expected to have specialized training. There have long been some who take the position that a person who knows his material can teach it without any additional training. However, in the lives of most of us there have been people who would qualify as experts in their own specializations but who made very poor teachers. Indeed, in the history of education in America, we find that the Latin grammar school teachers were often masters of their subject but frequently were very poor instructors. In modern-day education it is assumed that teachers will not only have adequate subject-matter background but that they will also have the specialized training to make them more effective in the role of classroom teachers. There is no consensus in America today on the exact type of training which serves best in this regard. Hence we find considerable variability of practices as we move from one state to another.

Undergraduate Program. Many teacher-preparation curricula are based upon the assumption that by the end of his freshman year in college, the student will be reasonably certain whether or not he wants to be a teacher. Consequently an undergraduate professional program is designed for those who are

20

preparing to be teachers. Indeed, in some states only those people who have completed such an undergraduate program are granted a teacher's certificate. Other states use a slightly different approach in which the teacher can follow a curriculum outside the college or department of education and then take certain education courses, either concurrently or after completion of the other program. In either case, however, the undergraduate student is trained in the area of his teaching specialty and also in teaching methodology.

Advanced Education. In addition to the undergraduate programs in teacher education, there are many opportunities for teachers to continue into advanced levels of education. Indeed, some states do not give full certification until an applicant has completed a Master's degree in a program related to his teaching. Other states grant certification at the completion of the undergraduate program but, by means of salary increments, encourage teachers to continue with professional education beyond the undergraduate level. This can take a variety of forms and can lead to a variety of degrees, depending upon the individual college or university involved.

Internship. As an integral part of a teacher training program in many parts of the country, students are required to spend a considerable amount of time as student teachers. This is considered a vital part of the specialized professional training, and in many cases students consider it their top learning experience in the entire program. More attention will be given to this later. However, in general it involves actual classroom teaching under the immediate supervision of a master teacher.

Some states consider that the earlier years of full-time classroom teaching constitute a part of the training period. In some school districts an unusual amount of supervisory assistance is made available to beginning teachers. Principals are urged to give extra help to the beginner. States that have tenure laws frequently do not grant full tenure to a teacher until he has served for a period of two or three years. This practice, in effect, identifies these earlier years as what might be thought of as a tryout and training period for the teacher.

There might be those who would question the necessity of specialized training for teachers. A realistic appraisal of the complexity of the task usually will allay such doubts. The story was told a few years ago of a parent who, although highly educated, had never done any teaching. She agreed to take over a classroom on a particular day when the teacher had to be away. She left a note for the teacher at the end of the day, saying "I don't know how much they pay you, but it isn't enough." This person had a great deal of knowledge but was lacking in the skills and techniques that make the difference between an educated person and an educated, effective teacher.

The teacher makes a unique contribution to society

Another attribute which we frequently associate with a profession is that it performs a service to society which is unique and essential. No one can question that such a service is rendered by lawyers, doctors, and, to a large degree, by teachers. The unique contribution of teachers to society could be described in a great many ways. But isn't it true that, to a considerable extent, the continuance of our society is in the hands of teachers and schools?

Skills Are Required. It has already been pointed out that teaching is not "doing what comes naturally." Teaching goes well beyond just telling, and the skills involved in teaching are quite different from those involved in many other fields of endeavor. The teacher achieves desirable goals through the application of highly specialized skills. These skills are not developed easily. A great deal of study, of practice, and of effort goes into the mastery of the skills that are used daily by the thousand of classroom teachers in America. These teachers are willing to make the necessary effort to equip themselves to make their own contribution to society. It would be impossible to say that one profession makes a greater or lesser contribution to our nation than another. However, it is doubtful if many professions are more vital to the maintenance of our way of life in America than is the profession of teaching.

Special Type of Personality Is Required. Not only is the teacher's contribution to society based upon the mastery of techniques and skills, it also is necessary that the teacher be a special type of person. As an extreme case, consider the individual who is willing to master the techniques but who basically dislikes children. Obviously, such a person would never make a real contribution to society as a teacher because he could never be a truly successful teacher. Further discussion of the type of personality required for the teacher is to be found elsewhere in this book. However, the teacher must be a person of considerable animation, a person who likes people, a person who is willing to work hard, and a person who is convinced of the importance of his work.

Type of Work Performed Is Essential to Society. In order for one to appreciate the unique contribution that teachers make to our society, he should try to envision a society in which there is no teaching being done. This would mean, of course, that each generation would be deprived of the benefit of regarding the experiences of prior generations. In the absence of teachers, there would be no laboratory for youngsters to use in developing their own skills in human relations. There would be little opportunity for the development of an appreciation of social progress because there would be little knowledge about it. A society without schools obviously would move forward at a very slow rate.

In America we depend to a large degree on schools and upon the personnel of schools, specifically teachers, to see that the heritage of our society is passed along and to see that our youngsters are in position to advance the cause of society. Indeed, it is said in some quarters that one of the greatest of all social developments in America has been the development of our school systems. It is important, however, that we see a school system primarily as the machinery which will permit a teacher to function in a desirable atmosphere. The prime ingredients are the students and the teacher.

The true teacher is a person

All of the professions make demands upon those who are associated with them. We know about the demands upon the time, efforts, and energy of doctors, lawyers, and others. Certainly, similar demands are made upon the teacher. Further, many teachers stay in the profession by making personal sacrifices, a true indication of their dedication to their profession.

Salaries Are Never High. There has been a considerable amount of misunderstanding in some quarters about the salaries of teachers—certain people feel that teachers operate on the ragged edge of poverty. This is an exaggeration. In practically all communities the teacher earns a wage which is adequate for his basic needs, although frequently it may not provide many of the frills that are part of our modern society. But considering the amount of training that is necessary for one to become a fully certified teacher, it can generally be said that salaries paid teachers are never high. This, of course, means that persons whose prime interest in life is to accumulate money would probably not be interested in teaching.

Salaries Are Frequently Determined by a Variety of Factors. In many industries it is possible to make extensive use of merit salary increases, such increases being based upon the amount of productivity which a person has demonstrated. However, measuring the effectiveness of a classroom teacher is far different from determining the effectiveness, for example, of a piecework employee in a garment factory. The difficulties in appraising the work of a teacher have given rise to salary schedules in which salary increments are frequently based upon factors such as education and experience, factors which are readily measurable. The truly dedicated teacher may on occasion find it frustrating to see that his salary increments are no different from those of a colleague who is less dedicated and indeed less effective. On the other hand, until better ways are developed for measuring the effectiveness of a teacher, there is little likelihood of general acceptance of any other system for setting salaries.

The Work Is Demanding. Think back on your own days in elementary school. Think especially of the rainy day or the day when cold weather or other conditions made it impossible for you to play outside. If you went to an urban school, think of those days when for some reason it was not possible for you to engage in active play. You may recall the problems this created for the teacher. Then consider for a moment the disciplinary cases in your classroom with which your teacher had to cope on a day-to-day basis. If you had occasion to know about it, think of the times when irate parents called upon the teacher. Unless there was a teacher in your family, you might not know about the amount of paper grading, lesson planning, professional reading, and other demands upon the teacher's out-of-class time. We should add to this the fact that attendance at summer school, teacher's workshops, and other professional activities were expected. Nighttime demands such as attendance at parent-teacher's association meetings you may not have known about.

When we add that continuous contact with elementary or high school youngsters in groups of 30 or more is extremely demanding upon one's emotions and a tremendous drain on energy and stamina, we can begin to see that the work of a teacher is very demanding. Indeed, in recent years the work of a teacher has become even more difficult as a result of the constant addition of new and important functions to the work of the school. The professional dedication of many teachers is demonstrated most effectively in the fact that they continue year after year to function at their highest potential as teachers in one of the most demanding types of jobs that society has to offer.

THE TEACHER IS AN INSTRUMENT OF SOCIETY

What is your own concept of the meaning of "society?" Some people view it essentially as a collection of social clubs. However, we usually think of society as being the community or the social environment within which one functions. In the broader sense, the term might be applied to states, nations, or civilizations. Certainly all of these influence the work of the teacher in one way or another. However, in America, the community within which a school exists is the society which builds and supports the school. Consequently, in the strictest interpretation of the term, this is the society of which the teacher is an instrument.

Schools and teachers must be in harmony with community

There is an endless debate in educational circles about just how schools and teachers should relate to their community. Some say that the schools should take a lead position and should serve as instruments to reform society or to rebuild it in different orientations. Others say that, since the school is an instrument of society, its function is simply to give support to that society within which it exists. You may have observed that a school that gets very far ahead of or out of step with its society is likely to reduce its effectiveness. Yet our society is not static. Consequently a school that simply reflects a society might very well be running behind in the long-range schedule of community development. However, we can be sure that a teacher will have little effectiveness as an instrument of society if he is in complete disagreement with the customs and practices of the community in which he is teaching. In the final analysis, probably the controlling criterion should be common sense on the part of the teachers. In your own experience have you ever known of a teacher whose effectiveness was reduced because of his tendency to ignore the community in which he worked?

The Teacher Who Never Changes. At one extreme in the spectrum of teacher-community relations is the teacher who started to work in a community many years ago and to this day is still doing the same things in the same way that he was doing them at the time that he started to work. This would mean, of course, that the teacher in question would still be teaching subject content which has now become totally obsolete. It would also mean that this teacher would be using methods which have long since been improved upon. In short, such a teacher would be serving a society which has ceased to exist.

The Teacher Who Goes Overboard. In every profession there are a certain number of people who insist upon being pioneers. These people are inclined to seize upon every movement, whether major or minor, as a "cure-all" for the ills of society. The teaching profession is not spared this phenomenon. One occasionally encounters a teacher who has, throughout his career, been in the position of championing causes, many of which were fairly trivial in nature.

You may have noted that the educational world is prone to look for panaceas. This is just as true for individual teachers as it is for the profession generally. Consider, for example, the high school chemistry teacher who learned something about the use of films as a teaching aid. He hastily collected a sequence of films which he used, not as an aid to teaching, but as a substitute teacher. This teacher operated on the logic that if some films were good, more would be better, and still more would do the job for him. Frequently such a teacher loses touch with colleagues, students, and community as a result of the ailment sometimes referred to as "overboarditis."

It should be repeated that the two types of teachers described above are examples of extremes, with one earnestly resisting all change, and the other seeking out changes to make, regardless of their merits. The most effective teacher is the one who takes an intermediate position between these extremes. Such a teacher is constantly on the alert for ways and means of doing a better job but is not willing to seize upon every passing fancy as the ultimate cure for all educational ills. The judicious approach is the only defensible way of dealing with educational movements. Only those teachers who use this approach are serving as truly effective instruments of their society.

The teacher works with youngsters as they are

A beginning teacher remarked that teaching would be quite if it were not for the students. However, the students are there and they are provided by the community which supports the school. Consequently, their needs are the dominant influence in the work of the teacher who is serving that community.

We Must Take Them Where They Are. Imagine a situation in which you are a sixth grade teacher in a particular school. You find that in the area of mathematics your class is doing work which would be about fourth grade level at other schools. At this point you must face up to the fact that you must take the youngsters where they are, not where you wish they were. If a teacher teaches sixth grade arithmetic to a class that should be having fourth grade arithmetic, he is going to encounter endless frustration. The students will be lost simply because the work is above the level which they can handle. Under such circumstances the community which is supporting the school expects the teachers to take the youngsters as they are and to work with them in order to move them forward from their present position.

We Must Try to Move Each Individual Forward. It is worth

repeating that teaching-learning is an individual process. Although we work with classes, a class as such does not learn anything. It is only the people in the class who learn. Consequently, the task of the teacher is to take his 25 or 30 or more students and work with them as a group and as individuals so as to move each person forward in the educational sense. Students are usually grouped into grade levels according to chronological age. However, they do not all begin at the same place, they do not all have the same rate of progress, and at the end of the year they will not all be at the same place. The task of the teacher is to see that each has had the treatment that will help him progress as rapidly as his own potential will permit. Having done this, the teacher will have served a very effective and useful purpose.

The teacher uses the community as a setting for instruction

The story is told of a teacher who worked in a one-room school in a community which was very hilly and eroded. The school was balanced precariously on the bank of a very large gully. A visitor at the school was amazed to learn that they were studying about soil erosion in an entirely different part of the country, with no mention of the fact that there was soil erosion threatening their own schoolhouse. While there are many phases of instruction that cannot be illustrated locally, the teacher certainly should be on the alert to make effective use of those that are available.

Reality Requires Local Applications. A writer in the field of elementary school mathematics has pointed out that one reason some students have trouble with mathematics problems is simply that such problems lack reality. Lacking reality also would mean that they probably are lacking in interest to the students. Students living in a wheat-producing area would likely have little interest, for example, in working problems about cotton. The same thing holds true generally. The greatest degree of reality available to the teacher in his instruction is the reality that lies within and just outside the school classroom. A resourceful teacher can find endless sources of instructional materials close by.

Many Teaching Concepts Grow Out of the Community. In

your own high school days did you ever go on a field trip? If so, was it used as an effective means of instruction? Some are used in this way; some are not. A high school class that had been studying the principles of generation of electricity would probably benefit from visiting the local generating station, assuming that the visit is properly planned and conducted. A lower elementary class visited a dairy and found it to be a fascinating educational experience.

Consider the community in which you grew up. Do you know the source of the water supply for the community? Do you know the system being used for garbage disposal, sewage disposal? Do you know the source of the electric power used in your home? The alert teacher frequently can make very effective use of questions such as these as a means of initiating instruction, not only about the community itself but about basic principles which are applied in community problems such as those listed above.

Ultimately the teacher serves his community

It is generally true that people employed by governmental agencies are employed to render a service. Such agencies are not designed for production of a commodity but are for the purpose of rendering some sort of needed service. Consequently the teacher, as an employee of a publicly supported institution, is expected to render certain services which are needed by that community. While some teachers might be reluctant to think of themselves as servants, this is the basic role which they perform.

It should be kept clearly in mind that rendering a service does not in any way imply anything menial or degrading. Frequently the teachers are among the best educated citizens in a community. As has been pointed out earlier, teachers are specifically educated to perform certain highly technical and demanding tasks, and consequently are in a position to render a type of service which is of extreme importance to society. In most communities it is recognized that teachers render effective and important service and they are highly regarded as members of the professional community.

Did you ever hear a teacher say, half-apologizing, "I am

only a teacher"? This attitude would be very hard to defend. After all, it is to the teacher and to the school that the community entrusts its most precious possession, namely, its youth. Consequently a person who serves in so vital a role does not owe an apology to any person as long as this role is being fulfilled in a creditable manner.

The teacher as an instrument of society serves his community in an honorable and demanding capacity. Most communities appreciate the type of work done by their teachers and accept their teachers as real community benefactors.

What of the teacher who cannot serve as an instrument of his local society?

In the earlier sections of this book attention has been given to the role of the teacher in his society. Some teachers find it extremely difficult to accept this role.

Make Essential Adjustments. Every community in America has its own pattern of life. This pattern might be very similar to that of neighboring communities, but in certain ways it will probably be different. Since teachers work with and for people, it is important that they know the characteristics of the community in which they work. Certain adjustments to these characteristics will likely be necessary.

Try a Different Community. Let us take an illustration from the area of higher education. A particular man had taught for many years in a relatively small, exclusive, liberal arts college. While he found this to be a satisfying type of work, he accepted a considerably larger salary at a state university. His community here was entirely different. The university had a liberal admissions policy. It had a large student body and the professional schools were strong. The professor in question found that the adjustments to the new environment were going to be difficult for him. After one year he went to another college quite similar to the one in which he had originally been employed.

This principle would hold for all teachers: If a teacher is employed in a community whose customs are difficult for him to understand, and if he cannot make the necessary adjustments in order to be able to work in this community, it is in the best interest of the teacher himself and of the community that he change his location. Continued employment under these conditions would probably lead to endless frustration.

THE TEACHER IS A PERSON

Up to this point our discussion has centered around the teacher as one who operates in a particular profession under certain environmental conditions. This section gives consideration to the fact that, while the teacher does hold a highly responsible position in society, he also has certain essential obligations to himself and his family, as is true of any other responsible citizen.

The early American teacher "boarded around"

The fact that the teacher is a citizen with all the rights and privileges of a citizen was overlooked for many years in early America. Indeed, the basic right to have a home in the community where one works was denied him. It was considered part of a teacher's salary that he be given free board and room. However, this was achieved by having the teacher spend a week in one home, a week in another, and a week in another. Can you imagine the endless adjustments that must have been required of such a teacher? Obviously this arrangement made it impossible for the teacher to have a true home. If he had a family, the home had to be established elsewhere. Frequently the teacher spent the school year separated from his family. It was a major forward step in the status of the teacher when some unknown hero in our profession demanded that he be given money in lieu of the doubtful form of compensation called "boarding around."

The teacher should have all rights and privileges due a citizen

As a person with an above-average education, the teacher is in position to serve as a useful and effective citizen in a community. Indeed, there is a twofold obligation implied. The teacher should expect that the community would grant to him the rights due a citizen, and the community has the right to expect that the teacher exercise these rights in a responsible manner.

The Right to Vote. This most basic of all rights is certainly due the teacher. A problem that the teacher sometimes encounters along this line is in the matter of meeting residence requirements. As a result, some teachers continue to vote in what they consider to be their home community, despite the fact that they may be teaching elsewhere. Probably the most important point to be observed is that the teacher should be a voting citizen in some community where he is in position to serve as an intelligent voter.

The Right to Hold Elective Office. Customs vary widely among the communities of America as to the right of the teacher to hold elective office. Some communities take pride in the fact that their high school principal is a member of the state legislature or that a particular teacher is a member of the city council. Others take the position that this is not good practice. In some cases there are written policies forbidding teachers to hold elective office. Probably in most such cases the regulation grew out of an unfortunate experience with teachers who held elective offices and who may have neglected school duties as a result of the demands made upon their time and energies by such offices. Other communities forbid teachers to hold positions on school boards on the assumption that such persons might be subject to "conflicts of interest" on occasion. Probably a majority of communities in America, however, would not find it objectionable to have teachers holding elective office so long as the office does not make too many demands upon the time of the teacher.

The Right to Adequate Compensation for Self and Family. When teachers get into a discussion, the matter of salaries will usually arise. Reports issued by the National Education Association and other agencies indicate that there is a wide variability of teachers' salaries among various states and school districts. However, a teacher has a fundamental right as a person to be compensated for his efforts and to have sufficient income to establish a home, raise a family, and observe a decent standard of living. This is obvious but is sometimes misunderstood in some of the communities of America.

The Right to Reasonable Degree of Job Security. The early American teacher expected to move frequently. A great advancement was made when various states and districts began to establish some patterns of job security in the form of tenure laws. The teacher whose position is in jeopardy is not likely to render his best service as a teacher. Also, as a person, he has the right to assume that, as long as he continues to function effectively, he should be able to look forward to a reasonable degree of job security.

The Right to Reasonable Degree of Job Mobility. When personal or other considerations make it desirable for a teacher to change from one school system to another, he has a right to expect that he would be permitted to make this change without any type of professional penalty. Of course there are certain ethical considerations involved. For example, a person should not plan to change jobs during a school year. He should try to avoid submitting a resignation just before a school term begins. As long as these ethical points are observed, a teacher should be able to enjoy the same type of job mobility that is found in other areas of employment.

The Right to Progress Professionally As Merited. In view of the complexity of the work of a teacher, it is sometimes hard to define the term "merit." However, in most schools there are certain teachers who stand out as being unusually effective. It is to be hoped that as opportunities for professional advancement arise within a district, these teachers would be given consideration. One hears remarks from teachers on occasion that "only coaches (or counselors, etc.) seem to be eligible for principalships." Whether this is true or not, the existence of such rumors can be hard on teacher morale. It is desirable to have a school system grant professional promotions solely on the basis of professional qualifications.

The teacher shares in the responsibilities of citizenship

There may be a tendency among teachers to place more emphasis on rights and privileges than on responsibilities. However, these have to go hand-in-hand. Hence a teacher who expects to be an accepted member of a community has to be willing to assume the responsibilities that are inherent in such a position. These responsibilities could be listed in fairly great detail. However, let us consider just a few of them.

Participation in Community Matters. Some problems that arise within a community are of such a nature that teachers can make an especially valuable contribution. For example, problems involving the youth of the community frequently are best understood by teachers because of their special training in understanding youth. Whenever community problems arise in which teachers can make a contribution, it is to be expected that they will be available for such contributions. It should be understood, of course, that these have to be kept within reasonable bounds so that they do not infringe upon the professional responsibilities of the teacher.

The Teacher Should Use Common Sense and Judgment. Especially in urban areas teachers have opportunities to affiliate with a wide variety of causes and movements. Many of these have high motives and probably serve useful purposes. On the other hand some of them might not. The teacher should not feel so flattered by invitations that he accepts them without looking further into the nature of the group with which he is affiliating. The important thing is that before the teacher becomes identified with an organization, he should find out all he can about this particular group. Then on the basis of common sense and good judgment, he should decide whether or not affiliation with it would be in keeping with his professional responsibilities.

The Teacher Should Not Use a Classroom as a Forum for Propaganda or for Promoting a Personal Point of View. A particular high school mathematics teacher was violently opposed to the use of tobacco. If she smelled tobacco on the breath of a student, she immediately dropped all considerations of mathematics and devoted some minutes to an oration on the evils of tobacco. The net result was that many students found the situation to be somewhat amusing. One described this teacher as "not teaching very much mathematics but teaching an awful lot of tobacco." Regardless of the merits or demerits of her personal feelings, this teacher was not living up to her professional responsibilities because she was using her classroom to promote personal opinions. At the same time she was diverting class time and attention away from the subject area to which she was assigned. The teacher as a person has a right to his own opinion on issues of the day, but he has to be careful that his classroom does not become a forum for the promotion of his own personal views.

QUESTIONS AND ACTIVITIES

1. In your own words, what is a teacher?
2. List the unique characteristics of the best teacher you ever had. How many of these characteristics do you have?
3. Some teachers become central figures in a body of folklore or legend. Has this ever happened in your community? What was unusual about these teachers?
4. Teachers have sometimes figured as major characters in English and American literature, both fiction and non-fiction. On the basis of your own reading, can you cite such teachers?
5. How active are teachers in the political affairs of your community? Civic affairs? Are they allowed to hold elective office?
6. Many teachers have also been ministers. Do you see any objection to such an arrangement?
7. Many beginning teachers have a wide diversity of job opportunities. What factors other than salary would you consider in making a selection of your first position?

SOME SUGGESTED READINGS

American Association of School Administrators, *Education for American Youth*, National Education Association, 1954.

Caswell, Hollis L., *Education in the Elementary School*, New York: American Book Company, 1942.

Conant, James Bryant, *Education in a Divided World*, Cambridge: Harvard University Press, 1948.

Dewey, John, *Democracy and Education*, New York: The Macmillan Company, 1916.

Hillway, Tyrus, *American Education: An Introduction Through Readings*, Boston: Houghton Mifflin Company, 1964.

Keller, Helen, *Teacher, Anne Sullivan Macy*, Garden City, N.Y.: Doubleday & Co., Inc., 1955.

Kilpatrick, William H., *The Educational Frontier*, New York: Appleton-Century, 1933.

Mehl, Marie A., Hubert H. Mills, and Harl R. Douglas, *Teaching in the Elementary School*, New York: The Ronald Press Company, 1950.

Prescott, Daniel A., *The Child in the Educative Process*, New York: McGraw-Hill Book Company, 1957.

Spencer, Herbert, *Education: Intellectual, Moral and Physical*, New York: D. Appleton and Company, 1869.

Van Dalen, D. B., and R. W. Brittel, *Looking Ahead to Teaching*, Boston: Allyn & Bacon, Inc., 1959.

Wilson, Charles H., *A Teacher Is a Person*, New York: Henry Holt and Company, Inc., 1956.

2

WHO SHOULD BECOME A TEACHER?

In our complex society one of the most confusing tasks faced by young people is that of selecting a career. Logically this involves three steps. The first of these is a process of gathering information about the occupational choices which are of special interest to the youngster. The second is for the person in question to make a realistic appraisal of his own aptitudes, interests, and abilities. Finally, he makes a selection of a career whose demands are reasonably aligned with his own abilities and interests. Have you ever known of people who went about career choices in a far less systematic manner? It is not at all uncommon to find cases of career choices being based upon hunches, fads, and passing interests. It is doubtful if many of these actually lead to satisfying careers.

A point of continuing emphasis in this book is that the work of a teacher is complex and that specialized skills are required. However, it would be an oversimplification to say that skills alone determine one's success or failure as a teacher. For example, can you imagine a person being a successful teacher, regardless of background skills, if he had an honest dislike for children or adolescents? The primary purpose of this chapter is to survey the attributes and characteristics of those people to whom a teaching career would probably be a satisfying experience.

HISTORICALLY, TEACHING WAS NONSELECTIVE

During the colonial and early national period in American history the field of teaching seemed to have extensive appeal to the drifters. Various writings, both fictional and nonfictional, deal with people who turned to teaching as a means of making a living after having failed repeatedly in other lines of endeavor. A person who was unable to do the physical work that was demanded in early American society often ended up in the classroom. It has been said that many of those who entered teaching did so on a "forfeit basis." This is probably a good description of the nonselectivity of teaching during the colonial and early national period in American history. Certainly it would be unjustified to refer to teaching as being a profession at that time. It was merely an occupation or a line of work which seemed to appeal to an extensive assortment of misfits.

The dame school

A peculiar feature of American education is that it grew from the top downward. Colleges and Latin grammar schools existed for many years in communities in which there was little or no provision for students to gain elementary school educations. In general the burden for providing such educational background fell to the families. The wealthier families depended largely upon tutors to teach their children the rudiments of learning. In other cases the parents themselves did most of the teaching. However, there is an occasional reference in the educational literature to a very crude form of elementary school during the colonial and early national period. This was referred to as the "dame school." This school was kept by a "teacher" who was usually an object of disguised charity. For example, if a widow was faced with the task of providing a livelihood for her own family, sometimes she would establish a school in her own home. Despite the fact that she might have had only minimal education herself, some parents, as a means of helping the teacher along, would pay a nominal tuition fee to send their children for part of the day to study with her. There does not seem to have been any minimum age for attendance. The result is that many dame schools were more like baby sitting services than educational institutions.

The teacher of the dame school normally taught in her own home. One can readily envision this woman going about her household tasks while at the same time giving passing attention to a group of smaller children who were engaged in pursuits only slightly related to education. Indeed, it is doubtful if the dame school should be referred to as a school at all, in view of the highly informal and, to a large degree, ineffective methods used in such schools.

Servants and apprentices as teachers

As you probably recall from American history, a fairly large group of people came to America as bond servants. Generally, these were people who desired to make the move to America but who did not have enough money to pay their passage fare. There were arrangements by which some individual or company would advance the money for passage with the stipulation that the immigrant would be a bond servant for a designated number of years. While the bond servant group included people with a wide variety of skills, there is evidence to indicate that some of them were schoolmasters. An advertisement that appeared in a Baltimore newspaper in 1786 announced the impending arrival of a number of healthy men and women servants coming from Belfast and Cork. Among the tradesmen included in this group were carpenters, shoemakers, coopers, blacksmiths, staymakers, bookbinders, clothiers, dyers, butchers, millwrights, laborers, and schoolmasters. The purpose of the advertisement was to announce the impending sale of the indentures.

Another source of teachers during the period in question was the system of apprenticeship. Actually the apprentice during the colonial period had a status which was essentially that of servant, although, of course, there was the obligation on the part of the master to provide for the apprentice's welfare and to give him certain types of training. We still find records in educational history of some of the contracts, or "instruments," by which an apprentice entered into the trade of schoolmaster. A case frequently cited is that of John Campbell, the instrument being dated the 18th of July, 1722. Campbell was assigned as apprentice to George Brownell to learn "the art, trade or mystery" of teaching. The term of the apprenticeship was ten years and three months.

The fact that servants and apprentices were engaged as teachers during the colonial and early national period of American history indicated that teaching as a field was highly unselective. One does not require too much imagination to envision the amount of enthusiasm given by these people to their daily tasks.

One can further assume that most of the teachers from the ranks of servants and apprentices were reluctant teachers. In the case of both indentured servants and apprentices, it was quite common to have them run away from their masters. There are still in existence documents in which masters of runaway teachers advertised rewards for their return. The same thing holds true for the apprentices. An illustration for this is an advertisement in the *Pennsylvania Gazette* in the year 1756. A certain man was advertising for three lost items: a watch, a horse, and a schoolmaster. In the part applying to the school-master, we find the name and description of the man, along with the statement that anyone giving information as to his whereabouts would receive twenty shillings as a reward.

There is some indication that certain of the indentured servants combined teaching with other types of work in order to shorten their period of indenture. In a society in which there was a tremendous need for manpower in all types of categories, this was probably a relatively easy thing to do. Hence we can see that the practice of "moonlighting" among teachers is far from new.

Ministers as teachers

In many societies other than our own there has been a tendency for people to combine the roles of minister and teacher. How-ever, this practice was notably true during early American education. Indeed, many of the best known teachers at the higher education level during the colonial period were of this group. Notable examples were Timothy Dwight, several members of the Mather family, and Jonathan Edwards. Usu-ally their primary work was as a minister, but in many cases they also did some teaching.

Ministers Were Persons of Some Education. In Virginia and Massachusetts the minister was frequently the most highly edu-cated member of his community. Also in both of these colonies there was a close relationship between the church and school. Consequently it was natural that many of the teachers, be-cause of their unique educational accomplishments, were called upon to serve also as teachers.

Church Pay Was Often Inadequate. Many of the ministers worked in small communities. Consequently it can be assumed that there were problems in ministerial support. Frequently the pay of the minister was not adequate for him to establish a home and raise a family. Indeed, there are indications that in some cases there was no salary at all paid the minister.

Under these circumstances, we can surmise that the minister would welcome an opportunity to do some teaching. Often he simply established a school for a limited number of students in his own home.

Can you envision problems that might arise if the modern school in the modern community were staffed to a large degree by ministers of a particular faith? Very likely objections would be raised by people of other faiths. Such problems, however, were largely nonexistent in the New England communities because, to a very large degree, all of the people belonged to the same church. Consequently they saw it as a logical thing for the minister to combine the roles of teacher and preacher. The minister's first obligation was to the church, while his work as a teacher was quite incidental.

Teachers who were enroute to something else

Another indication that the teaching profession has historically been relatively nonselective is the large number of people who have used teaching as a stepping-stone to another line of work. While many of these people may have performed at an acceptable level, they never really thought of themselves as teachers.

Many Taught in Order to Finance Other Types of Training. in a community where jobs were scarce and requirements for teachers relatively low, it was natural that many people who were planing ultimately to enter law, medicine, or some other field as their permanent line of work should turn to teaching as a means of acquiring money. Indeed, many prominent Americans were for varying periods of time associated with the business of teaching. Consider the case of John Adams. After graduating from Harvard University in 1755, Adams was appointed schoolmaster in the town of Worcester, Massachusetts. In parts of his correspondence we are given a rather clear picture of some of his experiences as schoolmaster. He continued in his role for a period of three school terms. However, during much of this time he was engaged in reading law at night with a local attorney. His work as a teacher ended when he became qualified as an attorney. However, the period as a teacher exerted a profound influence upon the life of

John Adams. After his retirement from public office, he once mentioned that he had learned more of human nature during his three years as a teacher than he had learned during all the years that he was an attorney, politician, and diplomat. On another occasion he advised young men that they should teach school for a while, for it was "the best method of acquiring patience, self command, and a knowledge of character."* There is every reason to believe that John Adams was a conscientious schoolmaster, but he was only a schoolmaster on his way to another type of work.

Another prominent figure who had experience as a teacher was Daniel Webster. However, Webster taught for only one year. He, like Adams, used teaching as a prelude to entering a different line of work, and we know very little about how effective a teacher Webster was.

Many Taught in Order to Earn Money to Enter Business. Among the businessmen of your own community, are there any who started out as teachers? Do you know of any farmers who financed their original land purchases through teaching? In nearly any line of work and in nearly any community we find those people who have achieved prominence in fields of work totally unrelated to teaching who started out as teachers. To them teaching meant a means of entering a business of their choice.

Teaching, the Royal Road to Matrimony. One person described the teaching profession in America as the world's greatest matrimonial agency. Many communities have over the years seen single men and women arrive to accept teaching positions. They have also observed changes in marital status shortly after arrival in the new community. Thus teaching seems in many cases to have served to promote the cause of matrimony.

It should be emphasized that there is no implied criticism of those people who have passed through teaching on their way to some other type of work. Indeed, if they found a line of work more to their liking, they owed it to themselves and to their families to make such a change. There is nothing about teaching that should shackle reluctant teachers to their

* See Elizabeth Porter Gould, *John Adams and Daniel Webster As Schoolmasters* (Boston: The Palmer Company, 1903).

jobs. However, the point that has been illustrated is that, in serving as a channel to other lines of work, the teaching profession has been cast in the role of a nonselective field.

Many teachers were misfits

It has been said that there must have been some type of selectivity in early American education, because so many misfits could not have drifted into this kind of work accidentally. While we can safely assume that there were many dedicated teachers in this phase of American education, records, both fictional and nonfictional, seem to give undue attention to those teachers who were socially maladjusted. There were probably several factors that contributed to such a situation. One of these was the fact that school terms were very short (frequently three, four, or five months). Salaries were very low. In some communities salaries were paid in grain or commodities rather than in money. The tendency of local boards of control to change teachers frequently, if not yearly, did little to promote the social status of the teacher. Consequently, the pattern in many communities was that a teacher would come in, teach in the school for one term, then move along to another school. Obviously this lack of stability would hold little appeal to people who were trying to establish homes. Hence, on a forfeit basis, teaching seemed to draw a large number of people who simply were not employable in other areas of work.

Some of the descriptive terms that have been applied at one time or another to the teachers of the period in question include the following: questionable private habits, inferior education, shiftless, itinerant, and poorly educated. Illustrative of this group is the fictional Ichabod Crane as presented by Washington Irving. In addition to the shyness and timidity depicted in Irving's writings, Ichabod Crane was so homely that his name is still used as a figure of speech in describing homely men. Do you find it strange that communities which desperately needed educated people would support schools and entrust their children to people who were such obvious misfits as to be socially unacceptable within the community?

**Why was teaching so nonselective during our early
national history?**

While a wide variety of factors probably helped to produce
the conditions described previously, several factors are readily
identified.

No Required Program of Training. Very few colleges and
universities existed in America during the colonial and early
national period. Further, no institutions existed whose purpose it was to educate teachers. The result was that those teachers who were available in most communities had acquired
only a haphazard type of education and were frequently products of exactly the same types of schools in which they were
teaching. Presumably the only way the teacher could be
trained in such an environment was through his own experiences after he was on the job.

No Certification. One might question the statement that
there was no teacher certification during the period in question.
In certain sections of the country, there were lists of characteristics which teachers must meet. Frequently these were noneducational in nature. In order to be awarded a certificate for
teaching, for example, a person might very well have been
required to affiliate with the dominant religion in the community. It might have involved taking an oath of allegiance
to some local governor or political unit. However, few of the
so-called certification procedures made major reference to the
educational qualifications of the teachers. During a later period,
the practice developed of having a teacher take an examination
before the school board which had employed him. If he handled the examination satisfactorily, he would be certified by
the board as a teacher. This situation was ironic in view of the
fact that the board usually employed the person first, then
gave him the examination and issued him a certificate. One
can hardly imagine a situation in which the board would fail
to certify the teacher who had just been employed by them.
It is only in fairly recent times that agencies at the state level
have been empowered to issue teacher certificates based upon
carefully prescribed lists of qualifications.

Not Particularly Attractive Work. In our society some of the
factors that would promote selectivity in a particular line of

work would be good salaries, good working conditions, and a great deal of personal satisfaction in the work. In our colonial period few if any of these conditions prevailed.

Consider, for example, the matter of pay. Some communities paid a very small salary to the teacher but did give him an option of collecting additional funds from students if he could. However, he was frequently enjoined from collecting from the poor and needy. In other cases, the pay was almost exclusively in grain, hay, or other commodities, with very little money being given.

Another factor contributing to the unattractive nature of teaching was the difficulty of the work. The colonial school was traditionally a one-room school. All the students were taught individually. Records indicate that the work day was very long, and working conditions frequently were most uncomfortable. Local community customs frequently contributed to the difficulty of the teacher's work, as, for example, the common practice in some communities for people up to twenty years of age to while away the long winter days by going to school.

Another factor is that the position of teacher often carried with it certain unrelated duties. Some of the contracts dating back to the period prior to 1700 indicate, for example, that schoolmasters frequently were required to be assistant pastors of the local church. Such tasks as keeping the church clean, ringing the church bell, assisting at various church functions, and even digging graves were sometimes assigned to the schoolmaster.

Another feature of teaching, which made it most unattractive to many people, was the previously described practice of having the teacher board around. This was looked upon as a form of salary and yet it denied the teacher the privilege of becoming a part of a community. The result was that if the teacher had a family he usually established a home in another community and spent what time he had in the area of his teaching assignment. In short, this practice made it impossible for the teacher to be accepted as a true member of the community in which he worked.

During the period of history described earlier, classrooms were frequently staffed by teachers who had failed in other lines of work and who had turned to teaching as a last resort. One would expect a very poor quality of work on the part of those who enter teaching reluctantly and who continue in it because they cannot think of anything better to do. One of the prime decisions you should make in evaluating yourself as a potential teacher is the very basic question "Do you really want to teach?" If your answer is *no* you certainly should continue to look at other professions as career prospects.

The decision to become a teacher should be based upon knowledge of the profession

A freshman entering college once told the college counselor that he planned to become an engineer. The counselor asked how he had arrived at this decision. The freshman answered that he had seen a movie about some civil engineers and he had been quite fascinated with the work they were doing. It developed that, outside of what he had learned in one movie, this youngster knew very little about civil engineering. Because of the extreme importance of a career choice, one certainly should collect all the information he possibly can about those professions in which he is interested before he makes his final decision.

Insofar as teaching is concerned, as a prospective teacher it is especially important that you know something of the nature of teaching. You might surmise that, having come through a school system and having had contact with many teachers, you know a great deal about the work. However, many of its aspects you as a student may not have had a chance to learn.

Every profession has certain special requirements which its entrants need to meet. What, for example, would you consider to be the personality requirements for a teacher? What would you consider to be the scholarship requirements placed upon the teacher? Did you know that some teachers fail because they lack patience with youngsters of the age group with which they are working? Did you know that some teachers are very likely to get into a rut and continue to do the same thing in the same way year after year? Did you know that a Master's degree is in many areas becoming a must for teachers? This list could be extended. As a matter of fact you could extend it yourself. The important thing at this point is that you be clear on the fact that there are certain special requirements which teachers must meet if they are to experience success in their field of work.

Another aspect of the work of teaching is its satisfactions. You may recall primarily the disturbances, disciplinary difficulties, and things of this sort that came up in your classroom when you were a student. However, most teachers have the satisfaction of seeing the vast majority of their students move forward in educational, personal, and physical growth. It is an endlessly satisfying experience to be a part of such growth. Indeed one veteran teacher summed it up this way: "If it doesn't pay off in satisfaction, it doesn't pay off."

Another aspect of the nature of teaching is the disappointments that go along with it. Many teachers have the agonizing experience of watching brilliant students actually rebel at the idea of learning. There are those students who are moody and who create problems through periodic defiance of the teacher. There are those who change attitudes almost daily insofar as their feelings toward schoolwork are concerned. Now and then teachers have the experience of seeing students get into difficulty with the law. There are always students whose growth patterns are a source of concern and disappointment to teachers simply because the teachers know that such patterns are not what they should be. Teachers are personally and to some degree emotionally involved in the growth of each individual student. Work of this type obviously carries with it a certain amount of disappointment for the teacher.

The decision to become a teacher should be based upon a realistic appraisal of one's self

Many of us are far more effective in appraising our friends than we are in appraising ourselves. Indeed some people can become utterly unrealistic in trying to evaluate their own personal traits. Other people such as school counselors frequently can be of assistance in this. There are personality and other scales and tests that can be used to help people in the process of self-appraisal. However, regardless of the instruments used, in the final analysis it is the responsibility of the individual to take a look at himself and to face the reality of his own strengths and weaknesses.

What strengths should one seek in himself as he attempts to decide whether or not to be a teacher? Most of them can be broken down into two general categories: personal and scholastic. There is a great variety of personal characteristics, and a complete listing would be impossible. However, a liking for people and a desire to work with people are most important for the teacher. In the area of scholastic strength the prospective teacher needs to consider first of all whether or not he has the basic ability to complete a teacher education program. Consider the case of a youngster who thinks that he wants to be a high school mathematics teacher. Yet throughout elementary and high school he has demonstrated little proficiency in the field of mathematics. Obviously he would be in scholastic difficulty from the outset if he went into a program which required that he take mathematics courses at a fairly sophisticated level.

In appraising your personal and scholastic characteristics you need to consider weaknesses as well as strengths. If small children get on your nerves, you should not plan to be a primary school teacher. If adolescents of junior high age strike you as being hopelessly silly, then you probably should not plan to go into junior high teaching. Or if you are the type of person who prefers to work with machinery rather than with people, you probably should go into some area in which you would work with machinery. Scholastic weaknesses should be considered in this same vein.

The decision to become a teacher involves reconciliation of viewpoints

Having made a careful study of the requirements of teaching and an equally careful study of yourself, the final decision whether or not to become a teacher involves the reconciliation of the two lists of characteristics. Some counselors suggest that formal lists should be written down. One such list would simply be headed: "These are the requirements of the teaching profession." Adjacent to this there could be another list setting forth the strengths and weaknesses, both scholastic and personal, of the individual student. Note, however, that the counselor can only serve in the role of helper in any such operation. The final decision has to be with the student. If after systematic study the student concludes that he is able to meet the requirements of teaching, he is then in position to move in that direction. If on the other hand the two lists seem to defy reconciliation, it is very likely that the student should look into other areas of career interest.

Some approaches that seldom produce good teachers

In our consideration of the question, "Who should become a teacher?", emphasis has been placed upon the fact that those who enter the profession should have a genuine desire to be teachers. However, a realistic look at the situation indicates that not all teachers could be classified in this way. As is true in most professions, there are those who become teachers for reasons entirely different from those outlined earlier.

Scholastic Misfits. Every college or university has among its enrollment some students who are constantly shopping around for a field of study that is more to their liking. Sometimes changes from one college or curriculum to another may be based upon academic difficulties within a particular program. Other such changes may be caused by emotional instability or simply a desire for change. Whatever the reason, there are always people who are continuously changing college programs. It is not at all unusual for such people to enter teaching-training programs. Indeed, some of them may become good teachers. This would indicate that they shopped until they found what they wanted. However, as has been pointed out earlier, good teachers seldom enter the profession on a forfeit basis. Some of the people just described doubtless do this.

Misfits in Employment After College. Just as there are drifters within college programs, so are there drifters in the postcollege period of employment. Consider the case of the young man who prepared to be a teacher but at the end of his first year of teaching, he decided this was not for him. This person returned to school and became a lawyer. After a year or two in this line of work, he once again decided this was not what he wanted. The next area might have been social welfare, business administration, or one of the more technical fields such as enginnering. Occasionally a drifter of this type becomes a successful teacher. However, most school personnel officers take a hard look at such persons before they offer employment. Doubtless the question always present is "Is this the job in which he will stay or will he merely pass through this on the way to something else?"

The Indecisive. The person described above was constantly changing his mind but was changing employment with each such attitude change. Another segment of our population is made up of people who simply have a hard time deciding anything, whether it be before or after college graduation. Such people have a tendency merely to drift. A case in point might be the young lady who ultimately became a teacher simply because her college roommate became a teacher. It is likely that a person who has difficulty making up his mind on whether or not he should be a teacher will have trouble making the decisions that are required of a person who is actually teaching. A truly indecisive person would probably find teaching to be a very difficult type of work.

"It is Not What I Really Want, But . . . ." In the matter of selecting a career, there are some very important decisions that have to be made. This particular point has been discussed earlier. Occasionally we find people who will look over the field of career choices and follow a line of reasoning like this: "My first preference would be medicine, but that is too expensive. My second preference would be engineering, but that is too difficult. My third preference would be law, but that takes too long. My last preference would be teaching." Certainly a realistic appraisal of one's circumstances in the light of career demands is to be encouraged. On the other hand, it is doubtful if we ever get very many good teachers who have put teaching "last on their shopping list" and have entered teaching simply because the individual finds that his

more preferred career choices would be difficult to achieve.

Those in the Market for a Meal Ticket. In view of the fact that teachers' salaries are not notably high, one might wonder if there is anyone in teaching who is primarily interested in money. While we hope there are not many of them, doubtless there are some. There are those, for example, who are willing to accept the modest salaries because of the relatively high degree of security offered by teaching. There are those who plan to live in certain locations in which teaching offers the best employment opportunities. Then, in a slightly different category, there are those who see teaching solely as a means of supplementing family income in order to maintain a higher standard of living. Certainly if a person starts out in life with a burning desire to amass great wealth, he is not likely to turn to teaching. On the other hand, there probably are some people in the profession who are more concerned with the monthly paycheck than they are with the personal satisfaction that comes from a job well done.

THE TEACHER SHOULD BE WILLING TO MAKE NECESSARY PREPARATION

Practically any type of work in the modern world requires a period of training and preparation. In earlier years, young farmers usually learned the work of the farmer by working with parents and family. Certain of the skilled trades have traditionally made use of apprenticeships as a means of training youngsters in their work. Teaching is similar to the other professions in this regard in that special training, usually a college education, is necessary.

Preparation requires time

A person who plans to complete the usual program in teacher education will be involved in a four-year program of study. Through attendance at summer school, this can be shortened below four calendar years. In some areas, the pattern now is toward requiring a Master's degree for complete certification.

This is usually in a five-year program. Hence, a person who plans to enter teaching is committing himself to a program of study that often will encompass a period of four or five years.

Preparation involves money

Despite the widespread prevalence of publicly supported colleges and universities in America, the college degree is still expensive. In addition to the obvious costs such as tuition fees, textbook costs, and others, there is for many people the added cost of living away from home. Indeed, this can be the most expensive part of college attendance for some people. There are a great many grants, scholarships, loan funds, self-help jobs, and other means by which students can help themselves in the matter of meeting college expenses. However, there really is no cheap way of going to college.

In addition to the actual cash outlay required in college attendance, there is the added factor of lost income which one could be earning in the time that he is going to college. There are numerous lines of work, some which are quite remunerative, that are open to potential teachers. Some of these require much shorter training periods than is required for teaching. Hence, in viewing the matter of costs, the prospective teacher must consider not only the matter of expenses directly associated with college attendance but must also consider the amount of income he is forfeiting during the time he is in college.

College involves work and study

In addition to costs in time and money, the would-be teacher should be conscious of the fact that gaining the required educational background also costs a great deal of effort. You may have heard college students discuss various curricula which they glibly say are difficult or easy, or which they classify in some other way.

The point that is commonly overlooked is that a curriculum may be easy for one person and very difficult for another. For this reason it would be impossible to classify a teacher education program as being more or less difficult than some other program which might be under consideration. However, if you will examine your own institution, you will probably find that colleges or departments of education have their quota of people who run into academic difficulties in meeting the requirements of their curriculum. Consequently the prospective teacher should be prepared to invest a great deal of effort in the matter of acquiring the necessary educational background for his chosen field of work.

Preparation never ends

One can hardly imagine any career in which, after a four-year period of training, a person could consider himself completely equipped for his entire professional life. Certainly that would not be the case with teaching. The prospective teacher should be conscious of the fact that the work of the teacher changes endlessly. Methods change, types of students change, institutions change, and society changes. In such an environment the teacher who stands still is faced with immediate obsolescence. Consequently a person who enters teaching must accept the fact that in addition to the initial preparation described earlier, there is the endless preparation which is required in order to keep him up-to-date in his profession.

THE TEACHER SHOULD POSSESS CERTAIN PERSONAL TRAITS

Can you imagine a successful surgeon who faints at the sight of blood? Can you imagine a successful architect who lacks the coordination required to use the instruments of his trade? While every profession makes certain educational demands upon those who enter it, it is easy to visualize the problems of those entering a profession who meet educational requirements but who simply are not the kind of people who can do the work required. Exactly the same line of reasoning holds for teachers. There are certain personal traits which are essential to the successful teacher.

The teacher should like to work with people

As has been mentioned earlier, the teacher makes use of many tools and facilities in his work. However, if anything could be thought of as raw material in the work of the teacher, it would be people. Consequently, it is vital that a person contemplating teaching as a career be sure he has a genuine interest in and liking for people.

Teachers usually prefer a particular age group. Can you imagine any two lines of work more different than teaching in a kindergarten and teaching in college? These are two extremes. It is not our purpose at this point to give detailed characteristics of lower elementary, upper elementary, junior high, senior high, and college students. Indeed, there is still another category. Adult education is a very massive operation in America today. A person who plans to go into teaching should decide quite early in his career which of these age groups interests him most. One young man who became a high school mathematics teacher was experiencing considerable difficulty in working with students of high school age. When an opportunity presented itself, he changed to an upper elementary classroom. This was an age group in which he was far more interested, and he experience a great deal more success that he had with the older students. On the other hand, a young lady who was working at the lower elementary level found that the emotional demands made upon her by small children were becoming very tiring. Consequently, she returned to college and qualified as an English teacher. She found a great deal more satisfaction in working with this other age group.

How does one go about deciding which age group appeals to him most? Have you had any opportunity in your own experience to work with groups of different age levels? This is generally considered to be one of the most effective ways of reaching a decision on this matter. Ideally every potential teacher should seek, through school, community, church, club, or other activities, ways to give himself contact with groups of children at various age levels. Such a person would then be in position to select an age group on the basis of his own experience. If such opportunities are not available, the person has to make his decision on the basis of what he knows about various age groups and, equally important, on what he knows about himself.

The teacher should be able to work with people

It may seem peculiar to you, but some people who like to work with people really are not very good at it. It is important that the teacher not only likes this type of work but that he is effective at it. This would involve a variety of factors. For example, the teacher needs to be able to gain and hold the respect of his students. Failure to do so can create endless problems for the teacher, the administration, and the school. Closely related to this is the fact that the teacher must be able to obtain the cooperation of his class. The teacher who is inclined to go soaring off into a cultural stratosphere while leaving his class in a state of utter boredom would probably get little cooperation from his group.

Another important factor in being able to work with people is the ability to minimize conflicts with and between people. A teacher who allows a particular student to "get under his skin" will find it very hard to work in a cooperative way with this student. Again, the teacher must be able to get people to work with each other. You can imagine, for example, a physical education class in which team efforts often end up in a squabble. Such unfortunate occurrences might well be caused by the fact that the teacher does not have the ability to get the students to work together. Note that this is somewhat different from teacher-pupil cooperation in that it deals with pupil-pupil relationships.

The teacher should be able to work with individuals

In an earlier section considerable emphasis has been placed on the word "group." This should not be understood to mean that work with individuals is unimportant. To be a truly effective teacher, one must work well with groups *and* with individuals.

Working with individuals can be quite different from working with groups. Some teachers are far more effective in one role than in the other. However, there is no escaping the fact that the teaching-learning process is individual in nature. Consequently, the teacher works with groups up to a point, but then very frequently has to work with individual members of those groups on specific difficulties. Did you ever have a teacher who was more effective in working with individuals than with groups? Or with groups than with individuals? Did you ever have a teacher who became impatient with a student who had trouble in keeping up with the class? Those periods when the teacher is working with individuals on specific difficulties can be the most demanding.

The teacher should have a wholesome outlook on life

To be effective as a teacher, one needs to be effective as a person. This type of effectiveness is usually associated with one's general outlook on life. A few specifics should be mentioned in this regard.

The teacher should not be a worrier. An elementary teacher who spends the day with 30 small children or a high school teacher who, in the course of a day, comes into contact with 150 high school students is never going to lack for subjects about whom he could worry. As a worker with people, the teacher is always going to have some students who are not measuring up to their full potentials. In short, if the teacher is inclined to worry, there are always some students who "need worrying about." Conscientiousness is required. Worry can only complicate the problems.

A teacher should not be inclined to moodiness or depression. A good teacher–pupil relationship requires that the pupils know generally how a remark will be interpreted. This condition cannot prevail if the teacher is a person whose moods change from gaiety to depression on short notice. Such moodiness would create problems for any person but especially for the teacher.

A teacher must be extremely patient. With 30 individuals in a classroom, each remark will be interpreted 30 different ways. This can require a considerable amount of repetition and correction of false impressions on the part of the teacher. However, a teacher who permits himself to meet such situations with sarcasm, lectures, or temper fits is not likely to get the desired response from the class.

A teacher should not be a rebel. As a member of a faculty working under a central administrative office, the teacher may on occasion be called upon to apply policies with which he is not in complete agreement. Such disagreement should be discussed with the responsible officials but not with the students. Some teachers have damaged their professional prospects by permitting a rebellious attitude to be reflected in their teaching. The objectionable policies were not created by the students; hence students should not be subjected to tirades about such policies. The teacher should be sufficiently adult to treat honest disagreement in an honest manner.

The teacher should have a true sense of values. Did you ever know an English teacher who was more concerned with the placement of commas than he was about the content of a theme? Did you ever know a mathematics teacher who was more concerned about teaching a step-by-step procedure than he was about teaching an understanding of a process? It is essential that a person engaged in teaching have the insight to differentiate between the important and the incidental. In short, the teacher should be a person of sound judgment and good common sense.

The teacher should be friendly but not familiar. There is a tendency on the part of some teachers to be overly concerned with their status with students. This can lead to a tendency to court student popularity. Such an attitude can give rise to an undesirable degree of familiarity between teacher and students. The teacher must be continuously conscious of the fact that he has unique status with students and that they do not expect or desire that the teacher be "one of the boys." A friendly and constructive teacher-student relationship is highly desirable. A familiar relationship can be devastating.

The teacher should be willing to work

Despite any comments you may have heard from the uninformed, teaching is not easy work. Let us consider some of the aspects of teaching that are very demanding.

Preparing for teaching takes a great deal of time and effort. There are such tasks as arranging for demonstrations in science, preparing for audio-visual aids for social studies, or ordering the essential supplies for an elementary classroom. However, one of the most demanding aspects is simply studying and planning lessons.

Even more demanding is the work of teaching itself. Did

it ever occur to you that a teacher is on his feet practically all day? This alone is very tiring. The process of instruction itself is endlessly demanding. The give-and-take contact with students in a class discussion demands a type of effort which would not be understood by nonteachers.

What happens after the school day officially ends? The work of the teacher does not end; it merely shifts into a different pattern. This is the time for planning tomorrow's work, for holding parent conferences, for attending committee meetings, for checking the endless flow of class papers that demand attention. It is hoped that there will be some time for reading professional literature. Also, this is the time for faculty meetings, a vital part of the operation of many schools. Thus, the idea sometimes voiced that the teacher's work ends when the final bell rings is completely erroneous.

In addition to the types of demands illustrated in the previous paragraph, there are many others. Some of these would be considered essential, while other would be classed as optional. The optional activities should be selected on the basis of sound judgment, with demands on the teacher's time and energy a major criterion. This means that the teacher must occasionally decline invitations to take on additional involvements.

Do such paragons exist?

In our attempt to deal with the question of who should become a teacher, we may have established a list of qualifications that would make one wonder how anyone ever enters teaching. Many people who enter the profession fail to meet all of the specifications mentioned earlier. However, through extra effort in their areas of weakness, they have built successful careers in teaching.

It has been stressed continuously that those who plan to become teachers should take a careful look at themselves in light of the requirements of the profession. Such self-examination will usually help one face up to his deficiencies in this regard. Then, during the period of teacher-education, he will have ample opportunity to strive for improvement in the weak areas.

In summary, the qualities that have been listed earlier, as well as others that might be added, need not be considered as qualities one must possess at the time of entry into a teacher education program. However, it is to be hoped that, while becoming a teacher, the individual can work to overcome his own personal deficiencies. In order to do this, he must make a realistic appraisal of his own qualifications in the light of the demands of the profession.

QUESTIONS AND ACTIVITIES

1. Can you cite prominent people in your community or state who were "teachers in transit" early in their careers?
2. If you were a school counselor and one of your students with a serious speech or hearing defect insisted he was going to become a teacher, how would you deal with the situation?
3. To what extent should the fact that "Mama is a teacher" influence a student's choice of teaching as a career?
4. This chapter lists at least five personal traits that the prospective teacher should possess. Which of these is, in your opinion, most important? Least important?
5. With reference to the personal traits mentioned above, which do you consider to be your greatest strength? Your greatest weakness?
6. During your own school career, did you encounter any teachers who, in your opinion, were in the wrong line of work? How was the situation handled by the school officials?
7. How many—and which—presidents of the United States were teachers at some point in their careers?
8. What would be your advice to a college freshman who thinks—but is far from sure—that he wants to be a teacher?

Bent, Rudyard K., and Henry H. Kronenberg, *Principles of Secondary Education*, New York: McGraw-Hill Book Company, 1966.

Cressman, George R., and Harold W. Benda, *Public Education in America*, New York: Appleton-Century-Crofts, 1966.

Elsbree, Willard S., *The American Teacher*, New York: American Book Company, 1939.

Green, John A., *Fields of Teaching and Educational Services*, New York: Harper & Row, Publishers, 1966.

Hillway, Tyrus, *Education in American Society*, Boston: Houghton Mifflin Company, 1961.

Kilpatrick, William Heard, *The Teacher and Society* (First Yearbook of John Dewey Society), New York: Appleton-Century, 1937.

Prescott, Daniel A., *The Child in the Educative Process*, New York: McGraw-Hill Book Company, 1957.

Woodley, O. J., and M. Virginia Woodley, *The Profession of Teaching*, Boston: Houghton Mifflin Company, 1917.

3

WHAT ARE THE EDUCATIONAL REQUIREMENTS FOR TEACHERS?

In many of the professions there are regional or national organizations that have designed educational requirements for their prospective members. However, there is no national agency that performs this function in teacher education. Consequently, although there are many similarities among the various teacher training programs, there continue to be considerable differences also.

SOME HISTORICAL BACKGROUND ON THE EDUCATION OF TEACHERS

Professional training never becomes static, since society never becomes static. In teacher education, changes are constantly under way. In order to understand the status of this program, it is necessary that we take a brief look at changes that have already occurred.

Early American teachers were frequently little educated

As was mentioned earlier, the widow who operated a "dame" school in her own home frequently was semiliterate. The same could be said of some of the itinerant teachers who moved from one community to another setting up short-term schools on the basis of purely local support. On the other hand, some teachers in the Latin grammar schools and some of those who were teaching in the colleges in early America were people of considerable academic achievement. They were trained as scholars in their field of specialization but were in no way trained as teachers.

Since the success or failure of the early American teacher depended primarily upon his ability to keep discipline, there was little incentive for the better-educated people to enter teaching. The youngster of this period received a minimum of individualized instruction during the course of the school day. This left him with a great deal of leisure time in which to get into trouble. Apparently many of them took full advantage of this opportunity. Consequently, the task of keeping discipline dominated all other activities. There was little about this line of work that would appeal to those people who had the abilities and training to work in other areas.

Another factor that probably lowered the educational level of the early American teacher was the fact that appointment of teachers was often based on factors other than qualifications. Control was usually vested in a three-man or five-man board of trustees. In some sections the prime qualification for appointment to a teaching position was that the applicant be the son or daughter of a member of this local board of control. The likelihood of employing the best qualified person in the classroom by this procedure was extremely remote.

Standards gradually improved

With the nation moving forward on a wide variety of fronts, it was inevitable that schools should improve. Concurrently with the upgrading of the schools came better teachers and better teacher training programs.

The Lancastrian Tutor. Early in the 19th century a system of teaching developed in London by Joseph Lancaster was imported to America. The method of operation was relatively simple. A group of older and more able students already attending school would be taught a particular lesson by the master. While it is believed that the subject-matter of these lessons to the monitors was chiefly academic, there is some evidence that at least passing attention was given to proposed methods of teaching the content. After having received this rudimentary form of instruction, each monitor took over a group of younger students and taught the same lesson to them. Of course, the prime merit of this system was that of economy. In view of the fact that one master could teach a large number of monitors and each of these in turn could teach a large number of other students, it is estimated that under some conditions one master was in effect handling up to one thousand students through this monitorial system. It is of interest to note that the monitors were given some slight degree of training in methods of teaching. Furthermore, they functioned under at least a remote degree of supervision from the master. Consequently, it can be assumed that the monitors learned something of the teaching process through practicing the art under some supervision from an experienced teacher.

Apprenticeship Became Common. We know that many of the trades in early America depended upon a system of apprenticeship for the training of recruits. Teaching was no exception. A person who was apprenticed to a schoolmaster served as an assistant teacher. If he was fortunate enough to have a master who had, on his own, developed certain skills in the business of teaching, then the apprentice presumably would also learn those skills. This system had little to recommend it, since the apprentice teacher had a status very similar to that of a servant or slave. He was entirely at the mercy of his master in the matter of training and even subsistence. However, despite its obvious shortcomings, the system of apprenticeship did provide some sort of training for newcomers in the work of teaching in early America.

Samuel Hall Founded the Normal School. The need for an institution specially designed for the training of teachers had become obvious by the 1820's. The normal school was the result. Incidentally, the word "normal" as used in this sense comes from the Latin word meaning "model" or "rule." It is assumed that the use of the term "normal" as applied to teacher training institutions implied that the training was to give teachers a background regarding the rules for teaching.

The first normal school in America was established as an adjunct to an academy operated by Rev. Samuel Hall at Concord, Vermont, in 1823. The fact that it was part of an academy would indicate that the first normal school training was at the secondary level. Essentially the students in this normal school took the same training as the other academy students, with some additional work relating to teaching methodology, keeping classroom discipline, and managing children. In the absence of any text material for use in the area of pedagogy in his normal school, Samuel Hall wrote a textbook entitled *Lectures on Schoolkeeping.* This book is of great historical interest in the area of teacher training.

Public Normal Schools Followed. Shortly after the founding of Rev. Hall's normal school in Vermont, James G. Carter opened a similar institution in Massachusetts. Carter realized that the task of training teachers was too big to be handled in the small, privately owned academies of his day. Under his leadership, and in the face of strenuous opposition, the first publicly supported normal school in the United States was opened at <u>Lexington, Massachusetts,</u> in July 1839. Others of the same type were opened shortly thereafter.

The role of the normal school changed steadily

As a newly established institution operating in a relatively unknown area, the normal school accepted students without regard to qualifications. The program of studies followed by these students was haphazard and poorly organized. Practically the entire curriculum was built up around pedagogical matters, with no regard to teacher competence in subject areas. Since there were so few of them, the teachers who taught above the elementary level were given little attention. However, as the normal school grew, its nature changed steadily in the direction of greater academic emphasis. As a result, the curriculum increased in content, and the time required to complete the course of studies was lengthened. The requirement that students have a high school diploma prior to entry was established. Consequently, there was a great deal of change in the normal school movement, especially during the last half of the 19th century.

By an evolutionary process the postsecondary normal school program grew into a college-level program. The addition of courses of study for secondary teachers required that more be taught during the period of study in the normal school. Certain national organizations became interested in the normal school. As a result of the interaction of these and other forces, many of the normal schools moved to three- and four-year programs at the college level.

As a logical outgrowth of the changes that were occurring in the normal school, the teachers college began to appear. The earlier ones were frequently called "normal colleges." Beginning in the latter part of the 19th century, there was very rapid growth in the number of teachers colleges in America. By 1900, many states had one or more such institutions. These provided four-year curricula and were degree-granting institutions. One of the great transitions in teacher education was when we moved from the normal school to the teachers college.

In recent years there has been a marked tendency for teachers colleges to change to liberal arts colleges. As a result, we do not now find very many colleges that are identified by title as "teachers colleges." Essentially, this means that the colleges have become multipurpose institutions, although many of them still have as their prime purpose the training of teachers.

Colleges of education within universities were established

Early in the present century a trend developed by which the major universities of the country began to be involved in teacher education. While there was considerable opposition to this trend, the movement progressed steadily. Consequently, most of the colleges and universities in the country today engage in teacher education through the organizational structure of schools, colleges, or departments of education. These are now accepted as an integral part of the universities in question and have made a great contribution to the teacher education movement.

Other teacher-training approaches

While it is not our purpose to give a complete history of the development of teacher education, it would leave a false picture of the process if we did not mention in passing some of the other forces that contributed to the training of teachers in America. One approach was the teacher institute. Frequently this took the form of a group that went around over the state giving lectures, holding demonstrations, introducing materials, and trying in various other ways to be of assistance to the in-service teachers. Another move was the establishment of summer schools within colleges and universities. These were designed to meet the specific needs of in-service teachers who could not attend during the regular session. Still another approach which came about through colleges and universities was university extension. Through this program, college level courses could be taken for credit by in-service teachers. The idea was to bring the university to the community instead of bringing the teachers of the community to the university. It had a tremendous influence upon the corps of teachers in America today.

Many of the types of work which were formerly considered trades have over the years come to be classed as professions. A major step in the development of nearly all the professions has been that of controlled admission. Hence, a major step in the progress of the teaching profession was taken when certification procedures were established to provide some degree of control on those who were entering this work.

Early Teachers Lacked Certification. The teacher in early America arrived at his post by a variety of routes. In some cases, the teacher simply advertised for students in certain areas. If enough responded to his advertisement, he was in business. In other cases the teacher was employed by a board of trustees, but frequently nonprofessional factors were dominant in determining the successful applicant. In the total absence of any type of certification procedure, about the only control on the teacher was in the matter of renewal of appointments. In the final analysis, any person was a teacher who said he was a teacher and who could convince someone to give him some students to teach.

Local School Boards Began to Certify Teachers. In early America each publicly supported school, regardless of size, had a board of trustees, the prime duty of which was to select the teacher. However, in the early 1800s some of these boards also decided to certify teachers. It should be noted that the same board that did the hiring did the certifying. As a matter of fact, as noted previously, they frequently hired first and then went through a certification procedure. In an account published in 1856, a teacher by the name of Alcott told of the procedure by which he was certified. After Alcott had been employed and all of the terms of employment had been settled, the board of directors sat in a special session as a board of certification. The applicant was required to spell certain words orally. This was followed by the assignment of repeating the rules of arithmetic. He had to display his handwriting, but, because of the stress of the circumstances, it wasn't very good, so this requirement was waived by the board. He was then required to read aloud from certain books. At this point the board voted unanimously to grant him a teaching certificate.

Mr. Alcott pointed out that the truly important things, such as whether or not he wanted to be a teacher, did not come up at all. He further pointed out that certain important areas of study such as geography received no attention because at the moment they were not being taught in the local school. The obvious weaknesses of such a system led to its ultimate abandonment.

States assumed certification role

During the 19th century many states created the position of chief state school officer. This position gradually grew into state departments of education. The creation of such departments meant that for the first time there were agencies in position to exert statewide influence on school operations. This placed such agencies in position to establish procedures and requirements for teacher certification.

Obviously it would have served little purpose if an official sitting in a state capitol merely decreed that certain requirements must be met before people could be certified as teachers. To implement this movement, state departments of education used the familiar "stick and carrot" approach. Certain funds were available for allocation to local schools. By making a distinction between the amount paid to certified teachers as compared to that paid to uncertified teachers, many state departments of education gradually assumed the role of certifying agencies.

Many local school boards were in violent opposition to the form of state control which they saw in the certification movement. However, after several decades of conflict, most of the local school boards grudgingly conceded to the state education agency the right to issue teaching certificates.

Teacher certification now generally a state function

Many state departments of education are now staffed with professional personnel whose job it is to evaluate transcripts and other documents in order to grant or deny certification to applicants. This has served to provide a high degree of standardization within the several states. However, there is still a wide diversity of certification requirements as we go from one state to another, but this has become less noticeable in recent years as a result of reciprocity agreements that have been worked out among states. There is likely to be further progress along this line in the future, in view of the considerable degree of mobility that exists among teachers.

A question might be raised as to how the matter of certification relates to teacher education. It is inherent in the situation that those colleges that are training teachers in a particular state will tailor their programs of teacher education to conform to the certification requirements existing in that state. Usually there is a continuous interchange of ideas between certifying agencies and teacher education institutions. Hence there has been a close degree of correlation between teacher education programs and the certification requirements to be met by graduates of such programs.

STATUS OF TEACHER EDUCATION

Since the time that teacher education came to be recognized as a legitimate function of society, there have been very few periods of total stability. The search for better ways to produce better teachers is an endless one. There is every likelihood that changes will continue.

Admission to teacher education programs not automatic

It became apparent years ago that a satisfactory program of teacher education could not be built using academic drifters. Consequently, under the leadership of certain national accrediting agencies, many colleges for teacher education have moved in the direction of selective admissions to their programs.

In many colleges, for example, applicants for teacher education are required to meet certain physical standards. People with sight defects which are sufficiently serious to impair their effectiveness as teachers are frequently advised to go into other lines of work. The same would apply to people with serious hearing defects. Applicants who are crippled to a degree that would hamper them as teachers are similarly advised. Especially important is the matter of speech. Many departments of education require applicants to take a speech test that is quite rigorous. In some cases people with minor speech defects are given a course in speech correction before their admission to the program of education becomes final. If the speech defect is of a very serious nature, such people are frequently denied admission.

Along with physical screening there is also academic screening. A student who is transferring to teacher education from another academic unit usually must have an acceptable academic record before he is permitted to enter teacher education. After his admission he is kept under continuous academic scrutiny. For example, many schools require the equivalent of a C average for student teaching. Since student teaching is usually required for graduation, this stipulation could very well make the difference between graduating and not graduating. Teacher education programs generally require the same academic standards as do other sections of the university and in many cases go above minimum standards in this regard.

Closely related to the selective admission policy is the policy of canceling admission for those who do not measure up. For example, it is not at all unusual for colleges of education to drop from their rolls students who have serious problems of emotional instability. Also if a student continually displays a negative attitude toward teachers and toward teaching, he is sometimes dropped from the college, since he would be a very poor teacher prospect.

As has been pointed out earlier, a teacher is a very special kind of person. The rising standards of admission to teacher education programs indicate that colleges and universities are trying to seek out those special people. There is every reason to believe that the admission standards in colleges of education will continue to become more rigorous in the years ahead.

College programs in teacher education

Teacher education has found its place in colleges and universities. Certain specific college curricula have evolved for students in this area. While there is considerable variability among such programs as we move from state to state or from college to college, they do have certain elements in common.

General Education. On the assumption that a teacher should be a person of considerable breadth of learning, many of the curricula require a large amount of general education courses. Indeed, it is not uncommon to have the equivalent of two or more years of college work devoted to the development of general educational background. This usually takes the form of certain minimal or basic courses in such areas as English, social studies, mathematics, science, and others. It should be noted that these courses are taken with students from all parts of the college and are not special courses for teacher education students.

Specialized Education. After a student has been admitted into a teacher education program, he begins his professional courses. This phase consists primarily of courses designed especially for prospective teachers. Frequently this begins with an orientation or "introduction to education" course. The basic content of this course is described by its title. In many curricula students then go into a second orientation course, this one being an introduction to either elementary or secondary education. The student selects the one that is applicable in his own case. Then the student goes into certain specialized methods courses, each being designed to help the teacher in working in the specific areas in which he will be teaching. In many curricula, a course in tests and measurements is required. The culminating course in most programs is supervised student teaching. This is sometimes referred to as the "payoff course." In this course the student actually teaches under the supervision of a master teacher.

We sometimes hear the charge made that students in teacher education programs spend all of their time on professional courses. Obviously this is not the case. In your own program, how many hours of education courses will you take?

Training in Content Areas. Students who plan to be high school teachers usually decide fairly early in their educational careers which area or areas they hope to teach. Having made this choice, the students are usually routed into curricula in which they can build up background in these areas. For example, a person who plans to be an English teacher would probably take some 30 or more semester hours in this subject specialty. The same would be true for students specializing in other areas. Again, the courses along this line are usually taken with students from many other parts of the college. Also, prospective secondary teachers take courses in supporting areas, such as adolescent psychology. Generally, student teaching is done in the subject in which the student has specialized.

One who is training to be an elementary teacher would do less specialized study, since the typical elementary teacher works with widely diverse subjects. Her curriculum is designed more for breadth than for depth. She, too, takes some work in supporting areas such as child psychology. Then she usually does student teaching in the grade of her special interest.

In summary, the college curriculum for teacher education students generally consists of three parts: general education, specialized or professional education, and subject-matter courses designed to build up competence in proposed teaching fields. Some programs depart from this pattern to a degree, but frequently such departures are in response to local needs. To what extent does your program follow the pattern described in this section?

Five-year programs gaining prominence

For many decades some people involved in teacher education have felt that it is impossible to produce the type of teachers society demands in a four-year program. Consequently, much attention is being given to the use of five academic years for this type of training. This has taken a variety of forms.

One type of person to whom the five-year program would appeal is the liberal arts graduate who does not meet the requirements for teacher certification. Such a person, holding a liberal arts degree, enters a college or department of education where he takes such courses necessary to meet certification requirements. This usually takes about a year. People who follow this procedure emerge with a single degree, since the additional year has not been in a degree program.

Another version of the five-year program is the one leading to the Master's degree—most frequently Master of Arts or <u>Master of Science</u>. It is fairly common to require completion of a research study as part of the Master's degree. Also, many schools interpret these degrees as leading logically into doctoral study.

Another degree commonly awarded is the <u>Master of Education.</u> In this program students frequently take additional course work in lieu of carrying out a research project. The Master of Education degree is widely interpreted as being terminal, that is, it does not usually lead to a doctoral program.

A third is the <u>Master of Arts in Teaching.</u> Some institutions have tailored this degree to meet the specific needs of people whose undergraduate degrees were not in teacher education but who desire to earn a Master's degree while working toward teacher certification.

Does your college have any provision for a five-year program in teacher education?

Programs beyond the master's degree

In their salary schedules many school districts are now recognizing the fact that teachers frequently go beyond the master's degree in formal education. One such provision is for a salary increment at the so-called "Master's plus thirty" level. Since a Master's degree usually requires about a year of graduate work, the "<u>Master's plus thirty</u>" program is approximately equivalent to a second Master's degree. In order to take cognizance of this pattern, many colleges and universities have established "<u>specialist</u>" degrees.

The <u>doctorate</u> is <u>truly the terminal degree,</u> in teacher education as in most other fields. This, too, can take a variety of forms. One such is the <u>Doctor of Philosophy</u> degree. In addition to a certain amount of course work, this degree involves a major emphasis on research and usually requires <u>reading proficiency in certain foreign</u> languages.

Of more recent origin is the <u>Doctor of Education</u> degree. Again, the pattern varies. However, in general, it is considered to be the equivalent of the Doctor of Philosophy degree but with a different emphasis. The Doctor of Education degree <u>frequently does not have a foreign language</u> requirement. In some institutions the research requirement is slightly different.

Many people find it confusing that students who are in a teacher education program are working simultaneously toward a college degree and toward state certification. While it is essential that the two patterns closely parallel each other, there is generally a certain amount of flexibility in the certification requirements.

Many college requirements exceed certification requirements

Those who plan teacher education curricula in colleges usually look upon the state certification requirements as being minimal in nature. Consequently, some curricula have considerably more stringent requirements for the college degree than for certification. For example, in one state the teacher can be certifield in high school English with 24 hours of work in this area. However, the state university establishes for an English teacher a minimum of 36 semester hours. This pattern is found in a wide variety of subject areas.

College requirements usually specific in nature

In many states the certification agencies list requirements on the basis of total number of hours with occasionally a specific type of course listed as a requirement. However, in the college of education curriculum you would probably find specific required courses. Also, certain other standards are spelled out in the college degree program which do not appear at all in the certification requirements. For example, a college might require a certain grade average in a field whereas the certification agency merely requires credit in courses in that field.

Generally, college requirements are related to certification requirements but very commonly are more stringent and in nearly all cases are more specific than those established by the certifying agency.

Ever since the creation of the first normal school some persons have looked upon teacher education programs with a degree of skepticism. The transition from normal school to teachers college to college to university has generally resulted in a higher degree of understanding on the part of nonteachers. However, there are always certain critics of teacher education who cling to the position that the only requirement for teaching is that you know the content you are trying to teach.

Isn't teaching "doing what comes naturally?"

Have you heard people say "you can teach anything you know?" Have you heard people take the position that there is no such thing as a teaching method? Yet in your own experience have you not on occasion had contact with teachers whose mastery of content was obvious but whose effectiveness as teachers was low?

A feature that is very often overlooked is that the teaching-learning process is extremely complex. A great deal of research has been done in this area but the number of unanswered questions seems to increase rather than to decrease. It is important that a teacher be conversant with the current information about how learning occurs. Without such information his effectiveness would be doubtful.

Have you ever had a teacher whose mannerisms drove you to distraction? Have you ever had a teacher who was so disorganized that he made class a painful procedure? Have you ever had a teacher who could take material that was basically interesting and make it dull? Have you ever had a teacher who, through misuse of good teaching materials, completely spoiled its effect? The basic difficulty with teachers of this sort is probably that they simply do not recognize the importance of the teaching-learning process. The chances are that more knowledge of and attention to the process of teaching itself would clear up many of the difficulties of such teachers.

A change of emphasis that has occurred in recent years relative to the process of teaching has accentuated the need for specialized training in the area of teaching-learning. Whereas early schools placed a tremendous emphasis on the process of memorization, the modern school places much more emphasis on understandings, appreciations, and other learnings at a considerably higher level. Overall the effect of this shift of emphasis has been very wholesome. However, it has created problems for teachers since higher levels of learning require higher levels of teaching. The higher levels of teaching require well-directed efforts, and these efforts should be based upon knowledge of how teaching and learning occur.

Existing programs grew out of need

American society is putting a tremendous amount of money into the education of teachers. The only basis for such an expenditure is that of need. If there were widespread doubt as to the value of teacher education, would financial support be continued?

As society changes, teacher education will also change. There is little likelihood that the present patterns will continue indefinitely.

QUESTIONS AND ACTIVITIES

1. The charge is sometimes made that schools of education require prospective teachers to take all methodology and no content. In your own institution, what is the methods-to-content ratio for prospective teachers of (a) English, (b) science, (c) mathematics?
2. How do the college requirements of your curriculum compare with certification requirements in your state?
3. Does your state make any provision for certifying non-degree teachers? Upon what basis?
4. Does your state have any teachers colleges? Did it ever have any? If so, what happened to them?

5. There was a time when some states certified people simply as "high school teachers." Do you see any objection to this practice?
6. How were the certification requirements in your state established? When were they revised?
7. What agency in your state administers the certification program?
8. To what factors would you attribute the fact that certification requirements vary from state to state?

SOME SUGGESTED READINGS

Eye, Glen G., and Willard R. Lane, *The New Teacher Comes to School*, New York: Harper & Row, Publishers, 1956.

Green, John A., *Fields of Teaching and Educational Services*, New York: Harper & Row, Publishers, 1966.

Heilman, Arthur W., *Principles and Practices of Teaching Reading*, Columbus, Ohio: Charles E. Merrill Books, Inc., 1961.

Hillway, Tyrus, *Education in American Society*, Boston: Houghton Mifflin Company, 1961.

Lundberg, Horace W., ed., *School Social Work, A Service of Schools*, Bulletin 1964, No. 15, Department of Health, Education and Welfare, Government Printing Office, 1964.

Van Dalen, D. B., and R. W. Brittel, *Looking Ahead to Teaching*, Boston: Allyn & Bacon, Inc., 1959.

4

WHAT IS THE STATUS OF TEACHERS?

The word "status" can be interpreted in several ways. Frequently it has a negative import, as in such terms as "status seekers." However, we shall use it in a more affirmative way. We think of the status of a profession as relating to the question, "How is it regarded in the community?" The standing of a particular individual in a community is usually determined by the person himself. However, it is virtually impossible for the status of an individual to be totally independent of the degree of acceptance of his line of work. As a potential teacher you should be interested in the kind of acceptance this profession has in the community.

HISTORICALLY, AMERICAN TEACHERS WERE NOT HIGHLY REGARDED

The status of an individual or a profession is something that has to be earned. Probably the reason for the low status of teaching in early America was that it simply did not merit anything better. There were several reasons for this.

Low standards

Educational requirements for teachers were practically non-existent in early America. Consequently, teachers lacked the type of status usually accorded to well-educated people. Another factor was that teaching seemed to be a haven for psychological misfits. Records indicate that many of the early teachers were sadistic and intolerant. Obviously people of this sort could not serve as a base for building community acceptance. A third factor was that many teachers were appointed on bases other than merit. Political appointments were very common, and this tended to reduce the status of teachers generally. Still another factor was the charity aspects of teaching. Some schools operated primarily as a way of providing the teacher with a means of support.

Can you imagine the degree of community acceptance that has been accorded teachers, in view of the conditions just described? In your own experience, have you observed any of these conditions in modern schools?

Low salaries

The early American teacher operated essentially at the subsistence level, simply because his community could not see any reason for his doing otherwise. Since school support came from within the local district, the schools usually were in a precarious financial state. This was reflected in the salaries they paid their teachers.

Frequently the length of the school term was directly related to the amount of money available. It was a simple case of operating the school until the money was all gone. Hence, the teacher's income was determined not only by his monthly salary but also by the number of months he worked.

Another aspect of the low salary problem was that it was common practice for a teacher to receive part or all of his pay in something other than money. It was not unusual for the payment to be in grain, in livestock, in the use of land or in the use of housing. The result was that there was frequently little relationship between cash receipts and the stated salary of the teacher.

Sometimes the teacher did not even receive the amount of money that had been promised. A case in point is that of Ezekiel Cheever. Cheever was a well-known New England schoolmaster who continued active teaching until his death at the age of ninety-four. His teaching career covered a span of seventy years. About 1688 Cheever found it necessary to write to the public officials in Boston pointing out that his pay was fifty pounds in arrears. This illustrates the fact that even teachers of high standing sometimes found it difficult to collect the salary which they had already earned.

It is implied in the earlier discussion that, if teaching was to achieve public acceptance, progress would have to be made in several directions. One of these was that teaching must attract the right type of persons; the other was that these people must be paid reasonable salaries.

SOME RECENT DEVELOPMENTS
REGARDING FINANCIAL STATUS

In view of the conditions just described, it was inevitable that improvements be made in school financing. Such changes have occurred over a period of several centuries. Let us consider the financial status of the teacher in modern-day America.

State support

A major change in the financial status of teachers occurred when government at the state level gradually assumed some responsibility for the operation of schools. For example, when school support was totally dependent upon a local district, salaries could vary widely between two neighboring communities. The so-called "equalization formulas" administered at the state level did a great deal to correct this situation.

Another result of the state support movement was an increased financial stability of schools. Old school records indicate that when school expenses were met totally within a district, it was not unusual to have a school term end quite abruptly for the simple reason that the district had run out of money. Indeed, under these circumstances there was no such thing as a standard school term. As a result of broadening the base of educational support, greater financial stability was achieved.

Another outgrowth of state support has been the development of salary schedules for teachers. In general, such schedules are set up on the basis of minima. In some cases minima and maxima are established. However, the presence of such schedules does assure that teachers of equal qualifications will draw comparable salaries within the administrative unit covered by the schedule.

Another aspect of state support is the widely adapted provision for systematic salary increases. Many efforts have been made over the years to develop a formula for such increases which would be acceptable to all interested parties. This is a difficult task. However, degrees held and amount of teaching experience are usually major factors in determining the salary of the individual teacher. Other factors sometimes enter in on a local basis.

Local support still important

As a result of the transfer of certain financial responsibility from the district level to the state level, there has developed in certain quarters an attitude of "let the state do it." This is not a wholesome situation, since the school serves the local community and should be a vital part of community life. In some states, state support can be used for operating expenses only. This places the responsibility for the school plant on local sources. Also in most parts of the country any school that has the financial resources to do so is encouraged to supplement state salary minima with money raised within the local community.

Salary status of teachers

Because of the rapidly changing value of the dollar insofar as purchasing power is concerned, salary data rapidly become obsolete. Consequently the National Education Association's research division continuously updates such data.

Summary statements regarding salaries would be difficult to make, in view of the wide variability that exists. In some areas unusually high salaries are paid. A case in point is the salary schedule in certain sections of Alaska. In a recent year, schools in Fairbanks, Alaska, paid America's highest salaries for classroom teachers. Other states such as New York and California have certain districts where teachers' salaries are notably high.

Since teacher pay rates are inevitably related to the wealth of the supporting area, we find that in some districts salaries are quite low. Frequently the poorer districts make a valiant "educational effort" and use a high rate of total tax income for school support. However, the actual salary rate is necessarily lower than that found in some other districts.

There is a general upward trend in teacher's salaries. In part this trend is based upon general growth of the economy. However, we would like to think that it also indicates a greater degree of willingness on the part of the American taxpayer to support the schools of his district, state, and nation.

What do you know about the types of salaries paid in your own school system? How do they compare with other salaries paid in your state, your region? In the nation? It is especially important that you be familiar with these data, since they apply to schools in which you might be interested in working.

Teaching still is not a get-rich-quick profession

Many factors enter into establishing a salary structure. Supply and demand have to be considered. The simple matter of ability to pay cannot be overlooked. Source of revenue is another factor. As result of these and other considerations, we find that there is a wide amount of variability among types of work which require approximately equal preparation. For example, a chemical engineer with a bachelor's degree would most likely get a higher starting salary than would a teacher with a bachelor's degree.

One reason for this variability is that publicly supported work is seldom in the top salary brackets. Teachers are, of course, dependent directly upon support from one or more tax-based governmental agencies. Hence teacher's salaries come out of taxes collected by such agencies. It should be mentioned that there are certain compensations to accompany this weakness. For example, teachers' salaries are usually not immediately affected by sudden or drastic changes in the economic structure.

Another feature that holds teachers' salaries down in some communities is the question on the part of the public as to whether or not better salaries are really necessary. This again probably involves supply and demand. Many laymen, for example, are inclined to oversimplify by saying simply that "a teacher is a teacher." The fact that some teachers are more effective than others and that the better teachers will probably seek out better salaries is not considered in such statements.

The salary situation in teaching has contributed to some degree of instability among teachers. In some communities there is a great deal of teacher turnover from one year to the next. Much of this comes about because teachers are seeking better salaries or better professional positions. It is to be expected that as long as teachers can move from one position to another with salary increments, many of them will do just that.

In examining the community acceptance of professions, comparisons are difficult and frequently meaningless. How, for example, could you compare an attorney with a chemist? Or a medical doctor with a minister? Obviously community acceptance goes to those professions that have a unique contribution to make. In most communities teaching has the status usually accorded to a profession that is making a valuable contribution to society.

A bit of history

The status of the teacher has undergone continuous change in America. A few decades ago, for example, certain communities demanded that teachers be paragons of virtue. One of the big assignments of teachers was that they "set an example" for the youngsters of the community. In order to see that this was done, many communities had self-appointed guardians of morality who kept the teachers under continuous scrutiny. Many practices now considered matter-of-course were frowned upon, while others were definitely "off limits" for teachers. This list might include smoking or dating on "school nights."

During the period described above, many teachers were expected to live in the community where they worked. Unmarried teachers lived in a teachers' home or else boarded in the community. The teachers with families were expected to establish homes in the community. Indeed, many boards of trustees stipulated conditions of this sort at the time a teacher was employed. Many of these same communities expected that teachers would be active in church work. This not only provided an additional community service but made it necessary that the teacher spend many of his weekends in the community where he was employed.

Teachers are now generally accorded treatment of other professional people

Gradual changes in society have eliminated many of the demands upon teachers described earlier. Do you consider it an

88

improvement in the status of teachers that they are now given more freedom in the conduct of their own affairs than was formerly the case?

In many communities today leadership roles are available to teachers but do not constitute an obligation. Hence, if a teacher is interested in a particular civic club and can be active in such a club, including serving in leadership positions, most communities would take pride in the fact that this is being done. Also, in every major community there are all sorts of committees, commissions and other bodies concerned with civic operations. Frequently teachers can make a unique contribution in such groups, and they are encouraged to do so. It is still true that many teachers are prominent in church activities, and there is no objection to such a practice. The important change that has occurred in this regard is that church work is engaged in by teachers as a matter of free choice rather than as a response to community expectations.

Did you ever know a professional man who was not regarded very highly in his community? Conversely, did you ever know a man who worked at a subprofessional level who was highly respected in the community? Community status is essentially an individual matter. Consequently, one's standing is determined not only by the work he does but also by the kind of person he is. Many teachers are granted a great deal of community respect. For example, some people respect a teacher because of his education. Many respect him because he is well known, or because of his continuous contact with families and groups. Others respect him because of his work. Most teachers who are accorded high status in the community achieve this status because they are respectable people working in a respected profession.

Many communities still object to teacher participation in partisan politics. Indeed some boards of education have written policies which explicitly forbid teachers to hold elective offices. Along the same line some communities object to teacher identification with extremist groups or with highly controversial causes. One school superintendent, when asked why his administration frowned upon such practices, answered it by simply saying "We feel that such identification reduces the effectiveness of the teacher." Do you see this as a reasonable explanation? What is your position regarding the holding of public office by teachers? What is your position regarding teacher identification with extremist groups?

SOME AREAS THAT NEED CLARIFICATION

In seeking its proper role in the community, each profession has to deal with areas of controversy. In an evolving profession the problems change, but problems are always present.

Better definition of role of professional organizations

Practically all of the major professions in America have affiliated organizations that are strong and active. To what degree is this true of teachers?

At the national level the largest teacher organization is the National Education Association. This professionally-oriented organization engages in a wide variety of activities and sponsors numerous smaller groups to serve specific segments of the teaching field. A smaller but rapidly growing organization is the American Federation of Teachers, a labor-oriented organization that has become very active, particularly in such areas as gaining benefits for teachers. Which of these organizations is stronger in your area? Why?

There are numerous regional and state organizations for teachers. These are characterized more by diversity than by similarity. For example, in many states the teachers' organizations are active political forces. They work closely with legislative committees in promoting salary schedules and other benefits for teachers. At the other extreme, some state teachers' organizations do little except issue periodicals and possibly hold a state convention once each year.

The role of the professional organization for the teachers is still unclear and is still in a state of change. A continuing problem for such organizations is lack of membership. Many teachers do not belong to any professional organizations. Until such time as these organizations have established their proper role, it is likely that problems of attracting membership will continue.

Leadership positions

In the ideal situation, leadership positions for teachers—that
is, the positions of principal, superintendent, and others—
should be filled solely on the basis of merit. However, those
who have observed the operation of local school boards could
doubtless cite occasions when other factors became dominant.
A matter of special concern is that sometimes the principal of
a school is selected without any communications with the
faculty as to their own choice for principal. Since these are
the people who will be working with the new official, it is
only logical that their voice should be heard in the matter of
selection. It would greatly enhance the status of the teaching
profession in many communities if somehow the point of
view could be established that promotion to leadership positions should be based solely upon professional considerations.

Less "moonlighting" would be helpful

Periodically we read newspaper reports about a person who
is a teacher by day and a policeman, bartender, or truck driver
by night. Usually such actions are justified or at least rational-
ized on the basis of salary problems. Doubtless there are situations in which, in order to maintain his desired standard of
living, the teacher must find ways to supplement his income.
However, combining the work of teacher with certain other
types of work definitely reduces any feeling of professionalism
on the part of the teacher. Indeed, one wonders with which
of his jobs the teacher is identifying under these conditions.
Incidentally, the problem of "moonlighting" among teachers
is not new, as has been mentioned. The early American teacher
frequently combined teaching with some other type of work
in order to maintain a subsistence-level income.

More public understanding of teachers needed

You might wonder if it is possible for the public to mis-
understand the work of the teacher in view of the day-to-day
contact between the teacher and the public he serves. However, many misunderstandings do exist.

Consider, for example, the short work day. Many people
assume that the teacher works only from nine o'clock until

three o'clock. Of course one who is familiar with the work of the teacher knows that this period is merely the student-contact period and that the work day frequently continues far into the night.

Then there is the three months' "vacation." Most people interpret "vacation" to mean a period without work but with continuing income. In these terms our three months would be more in the line of a "lay-off." Indeed, to those with family responsibilities the three-month period in each year in which there is no assured income merely constitutes a recurring problem.

One reason for public misunderstanding of teachers is the tendency on the part of teachers to socialize only with each other. It would be a very wholesome thing if teachers would look for opportunities to maintain contact with people in entirely different lines of endeavor. This would help in the matter of public understanding.

Salary based upon merit widely discussed

Many people speak critically of salary schedules which are based essentially upon experience and degrees held. Such people say that there should be some system of merit salary increases in addition to the automatic ones mentioned above. In theory the merit increase sounds very attractive. Furthermore, in some lines of work it has been found to be extremely effective. However, when it has been tried in the teaching profession it has frequently created problems. As has been mentioned before, the work of the teacher is very difficult to define. It is even more difficult to classify a teacher on a "success scale" in view of the abstract nature of that which he is trying to do. Consequently some school systems that have tried the merit system have abandoned it as unworkable.

More educational opportunities for in-service teachers needed

Public acceptance of a profession is intimately related to the efforts made by that profession for upgrading its members. This has been a problem with teachers. In some states teacher certification is for life. Consequently, a teacher who has once met the certification requirements is under no particular pressure to upgrade or in any way improve upon his professional competence. This type of teacher, continuing to do things in exactly the same way year after year, does little to promote public acceptance of teachers.

In some areas a great deal of effort is being devoted to providing in-service opportunities for teachers. University extension classes are widely used in this way. Locally sponsored workshops and preschool conferences are used. Faculty study groups within a particular school faculty have been very helpful. Frequently professional consultants are brought in to assist in such groups. Also, many schools are establishing professional libraries for their teachers. Under these conditions, the teacher is able to benefit from current periodicals and newer professional books in his area. However, despite the best efforts of many school districts, some teachers insist upon becoming obsolete as rapidly as possible.

What is the status of teachers in your own community? Are they considered to be professional people? Do members of the community have real understanding of the work of the teacher? What steps could be taken in your own community to promote the professional standing of teachers?

QUESTIONS AND ACTIVITIES

1. What in-service educational opportunities are available to teachers of your community?
2. How would you describe the financial status of the teachers of your community? Your state?
3. Would you say that appointments to leadership positions in your schools are based solely on merit? Explain.
4. To what degree do the teachers you know engage in "moonlighting?" Do you think this practice should be forbidden as a matter of policy?
5. Can you find any fairly recent articles dealing with merit salary increases for teachers? What is your own feeling about this practice?

6. Are the teachers of your community accorded the status of "professional people?" Explain.

SOME SUGGESTED READINGS

Barzun, Jacques, *Teacher in America*, Boston: Little, Brown and Company, 1945.

Butts, R. Freeman, and Lawrence A. Cremin, *A History of Education in American Culture*, New York: Henry Holt and Company, Inc., 1953.

Caswell, Hollis L., *Education in the Elementary School*, New York: American Book Company, 1942.

Gould, Elizabeth P., *Ezekiel Cheever, Schoolmaster*, Boston: The Palmer Company, 1904.

United States Department of Health, Education and Welfare, *Profile of ESEA, the Elementary and Secondary Education Act of 1965*, Government Printing Office, 1967.

Van Dalen, D. B., and R. W. Brittel, *Looking Ahead to Teaching*, Boston: Allyn & Bacon, Inc., 1959.

5

WHAT ARE SOME DECISIONS FOR THE TEACHER?

This textbook is designed to provide information for those who are partially committed to teaching as a career or who are definitely interested in such a career. However, after a person decides to enter teaching, many further decisions need to be made. Some of these will come after he has begun teaching. However, it is not too early at this point to begin giving some thought to them.

WHAT LEVEL OR AGE GROUP?

After you decide to be a teacher, probably the next most important decision is what you shall teach and to whom you shall teach it. Few people could claim to be equally effective with all age groups. Consequently, the decision as to the level of teaching can make the difference between satisfaction and dissatisfaction in a teaching position.

Elementary grades

For many years the elementary school consisted of grades one through eight. However, with the rapid development of the junior high school, we find that in most areas the elementary grades are one through six.

From the standpoint of job opportunity, elementary education has much to offer, since according to the National Education Association's annual survey of supply and demand, there is practically always a shortage of well-qualified people in this area.

What are some of the characteristics of the elementary grade teacher?

Must Be Interested in Working with Smaller Children. It takes a special kind of person to work in close personal contact with small children for a full school day, day after day. The emotional demands made upon such a teacher are tremendous. Even the physical demands of such work are considerable. However, many elementary school teachers derive from their work the type of personal satisfaction which would not be available to them in any other type of teaching. Obviously, the person to whom elementary teaching will appeal is interested in working with smaller children.

Must Be Willing to Develop Many Methods. How many different teaching methods do you see used by your college teachers? Now think back on your high school career. How much change in methodology occurred from day to day in your classes in mathematics, science, or English? Now look even farther back to your elementary school days. Do you remember that the methods of doing things underwent constant change?

One characteristic of younger children is a relatively short attention span. They get bored easily. Under these circumstances, they become restless and inattentive, frequently creating problems for the teacher. This means that the teacher can never get very well settled into a routine of life. She has to be continuously looking for ways of changing approaches and procedures so as to make them more appealing to her class. This would be a real chore to a person who loves routine.

Must Be Willing to Teach in Many Subject Areas. While some experimentation is under way in team teaching and in various forms of departmentalization, the dominant pattern still is for an elementary school teacher to teach a class of students in all subjects. Some schools have special teachers in areas such as music and art, but many schools do not provide such services. While it is doubtful that you could claim to be equally interested or equally effective in all areas, still you will likely teach all subjects. Obviously this would not appeal to a person whose preference is for a fairly intensive specialization in one or two subjects.

Must Be Willing to Meet Emotional Demands. Many of us have doubtless forgotten the tremendous emotional shock that is involved when a small child makes the transition from home to school. Indeed, this transition sometimes requires several years before the child is fully acclimatized. During this time, it is expected that the teacher assist the youngster in making this change. This frequently is a very demanding role for the teacher. Sometimes there are students who have special types of problems, such as unhappy home environments. These problems and many others make their own special types of demands on the teacher. Obviously, a person who is to fill this role should be one with a high degree of emotional stability.

Must Be Observant. Many elementary classroom groups

involve some children who need specialized professional help of one sort or another. This might include medical treatment, psychiatric treatment, or the type of assistance rendered by certain social or welfare agencies. The modern school will usually have available such referral services. The teacher needs to be especially observant for those students whose needs cannot be met by services normally provided within the school. The handling of such students requires that the teacher know the needs, the services available, and the accepted channels for handling referrals.

Junior high school

Again, there is some variability as to what is called a junior high school. However, the most common pattern is to include grades 7, 8, and 9. In some states, teachers are trained and certified specifically for junior high school work. In others, junior high school teachers are drawn from upper elementary and high school ranks.

A decision to become a junior high school teacher should be based upon knowledge of the type of work involved.

Must Know Adolescents. Adolescence is a period of transition from childhood to adulthood. Frequently, transitions involve confusion. Adolescence is no exception. You will presumably have courses dealing specifically with the phenomenon of adolescence.

The junior high school student is frequently hard to understand because of moodiness. A remark which, at an earlier age, he would have found funny may hurt the feelings of the adolescent. A topic which he finds fascinating can, in a matter of moments, become unspeakably dull. Likes and dislikes of individuals come and go. At one moment he is a child; at another, he is an adult; sometimes he tries to be both at once. In short, for many youngsters, adolescence is a period of confusion. It would be very difficult for a teacher to work with groups of adolescents unless he has some understanding of them.

Must Be Interested in Working with Adolescents. It is one thing to know about adolescents; it is quite a different thing to be interested in working with them. The rapid changes described

100

What
Are Some
Decisions
for the
Teacher?

above could be most irritating to a person who has little real interest in working with teen-agers. However, to another person, who has a sympathetic attitude, this same group would be challenging and even fascinating. Knowing about adolescence is essentially a matter of study and observation. Working on a constructive basis with adolescents is a far more difficult task.

Must Be Willing to Do Some Specializing. One of the changes generally associated with entering junior high school is that the student gets his first contact with departmentalization. This means, of course, that most of the teachers will be working in subject area specialties. Hence they will be considered, at least by students, as specialists. It is not uncommon to find a junior high school teacher working in two related fields such as mathematics-science or language arts-social studies. The specific impact on the teacher is that he is more specialized than would be the case if he were in a self-contained elementary classroom.

Must Vary Methodology. You would expect that adolescents would have a longer attention span than younger children. In general this is true. However, junior high school students are still not sufficiently adult to engage in a single type of activity for a full class period. The teacher must be willing to change his methods of operation at regular intervals if he is to hold the attention of a junior high school class.

Senior high school

In most patterns of organization, the senior high school consists of grades 10, 11, and 12. A person who plans to teach at this level is very likely to be teaching in a departmentalized situation with students who are adult in many of their ways of responding. As you have observed in growing up, each age group has its own unique characteristics. For example, a senior high school student is not likely to demonstrate the willful moods of adolescents. However, he is dealing with different types of problems. For one thing, many of these students are beginning to think seriously about vocational choices. This frequently involves the teacher. Also, they are concerned with social problems—problems related to dating, to student activities in the school, to school functions, and

101

What
Are Some
Decisions
for the
Teacher?

others. Many students in this age group begin to hold part-time jobs. Problems associated with college admission become very real. The teacher who plans to work at this level must be interested in the problems of this age group.

Must Be Willing to Specialize in One or Two Areas. With the exception of a few isolated instances, the American high school is a departmentalized institution. This means that it is likely each teacher will work in one or two areas. It is important that a decision be made along this line quite early. You will find in the teacher education program at your own institution that you are expected to build up a strong subject background in your proposed area of work. This can only be done after you reach a decision as to your area of specialization.

Must Be Able to Adapt to Wide Range of Ability. Every teacher at every grade level must cope with a range of ability among his students. However, if you think about it for a moment, you would expect that the range would become wider as students become older. Consequently, the typical high school teacher has to deal with students whose abilities are spread over a very wide spectrum. This requires a considerable degree of adaptation on his part.

Must Be Willing to Function in Informal Advisory Roles. A prime need of a certain type of high school student is an adult to whom he can confide his problems. Peculiarly, many students cannot establish this kind of relationship with a parent. The result is that frequently such students will select a particular high school teacher and will turn to him for all sorts of advice, personal and scholastic. This kind of communication is of vital importance to the student. A teacher must be willing to function in this role if he is to be truly effective in all aspects of high school work.

Post-high school

The field of adult education has undergone phenomenal growth in recent years. There is little indication that this growth has now stabilized. Consequently, adult education offers a tremendous number of opportunities. In setting up your long-range professional goals you should seriously consider the opportunities to be found in this area.

Must Be Interested in Working with Adults. Did it ever occur

102

What
Are Some
Decisions
for the
Teacher?

to you that adults might be less interesting to teach than children or adolescents would be? Many people find this to be true. Certainly, adults are less responsive, more self-reliant, and make fewer demands on the teacher. Yet working with adults can be very satisfying to one whose interests lie in this direction.

Must Be Willing to Specialize. There is little place in adult education programs for what might be termed an educational generalist such as the typical elementary school teacher. Adult students have little patience with the teacher who is not adequately specialized in his area of work. The person who goes into adult education should have a well-rounded education. On the other hand, he must be willing to take a particular subject area and build up a high degree of competence in it.

Many Types of Work Require Advanced Degrees. Whereas a person can usually enter elementary or secondary school teaching with a Bachelor's or four-year degree, this frequently is not possible in certain adult education programs. A person who is seriously considering a career in adult education should look quite early into the specialized requirements of the area in which he plans to work.

Several Areas Available. Teaching in post-high school areas can take a variety of directions. For example, there is the area of trades and vocations. Many school systems operate trade schools or technical schools as part of their regular program. Also, many industries operate training divisions to train their own workmen in new skills that are being developed. Numerous governmental agencies are active in this type of training. It is a large and rapidly growing field.

Another area of post-high school education which is undergoing rapid growth is that of the junior college. This is a multipurpose institution in which a student can take the first two years of a degree program or can go into specialties of a terminal nature. This type of institution will offer numerous opportunities for employment in the years ahead.

Senior colleges and universities are constantly in the market for well-qualified faculty members. The creation of new institutions and the rapid enrollment growths in existing institutions have served to create tremendous personnel demands at this level of education. At this point is should be repeated that work in colleges and universities will probably require that you hold one or more advanced degrees. Consequently, you should be willing to stay in school for a longer period of time than would be necessary for some other types of teaching.

WHAT LONG-RANGE GOALS SHOULD ONE CONSIDER?

We have already examined some of the major decisions that the prospective teacher needs to make. You will note that many of these decisions have to do with events and prospects which lie several years in the future. For example, your decision to become an elementary school teacher will not get you into an elementary school classroom for some years to come. How far ahead should one attempt to look into such matters? Or, from the opposite point of view, is there anything to be gained by not looking ahead? During the time that you are pursuing an undergraduate program in teacher education you will have unique opportunities to appraise yourself in the light of long-range possibilities in the educational field. consequently, this section has to do with long-range goals which should be considered by teacher education students.

Of course one question of long-term impact is: Do you want to continue throughout your career as a classroom teacher? There is a great deal of argument in favor of this course of action. Consequently, in considering some other possibilities, we do not intend in any way to imply that a classroom assignment is merely a way station on the road to some other type of work. Indeed, the classroom teacher enjoys a type of personal satisfaction which is probably not to be found in any other educationally related job.

Administration

Every organization has to have people charged with the responsibility of making it work. Education is big business. Hence educational administration is a big field.

Do You Have Requisite Special Skills?   School administration is a complex area primarily because it deals with complex subjects, specifically people. Consequently, the school administrator must be a skilled in working with people. The concept

104

What
Are Some
Decisions
for the
Teacher?

of the school administrator as a semimilitary figure who issues orders and has them carried out instantly has little basis in fact. The modern school administrator tries to achieve his goals through leadership, democratic processes, and skill in work with people. Which of these two approaches do you think would be simpler to use? In the long run which do you think would be more effective?

Another important skill for a school administrator is that of making and applying policies. The general guidelines by which an organization functions have to be established and carried out through the school administrator. The principal of a large high school or the superintendent in a large school district makes policy decisions every day. Frequently these have to be made on short notice. They have to be based on existing policies, and they have to be of such a nature that they will not establish troublesome precedents for future operations. They have to be fair and they have to get the job done. Obviously, it takes a special kind of person to be able to cope with this type of situation.

Also, the school administrator must be able to make decisions. Have you ever known a person who spends so much time deciding how to handle a situation that the situation is changed before he arrives at a decision? Some people can agonize over minute points. Others postpone decisions so long that they lose their effectiveness. A principal in his day-to-day relationships with students, parents, teachers, other administrators, and the general public must be making decisions constantly. The ability to make decisions is a characteristic vital to the successful school administrator.

Do You Have Requisite Special Interests? The ability to handle a type of job is not necessarily correlated with an interest in doing the job. Thus it is in administration. Observe the case of the principal mentioned above. The primary work of the principal involves the students on the one hand and the teachers on the other hand. Frequently it is necessary for him to serve as a channel of communication between the two. Also, problems in community relations and in other areas have already been mentioned. The good principal is the man who is specifically interested in doing this kind of work. Regardless of how skillful he might be in it, if it does not hold

105

What
Are Some
Decisions
for the
Teacher?

special interest for him, he will not find in his work the degree of satisfaction that one should get from a position of this type.

Another special type of position is that of superintendent. The superintendent works primarily with the principals and with the school board. He, too, is in continuous contact with the public and various special-interest groups. Certain unique characteristics are required in order for one to work successfully with the school board. If a person is not interested in this kind of work, he probably would not develop any real proficiency in working with a lay board of control such as the ordinary school board. Consequently, if you, on a long-range basis, think you might be interested in school administration, you should consider very seriously whether or not you have the special skills and interests which would be necessary in order to make this a satisfying educational career.

Supervision

The supervisor frequently works closely with the superintendent but his responsibilities lie in a different direction. The supervisor's prime concern should be in helping or promoting good instruction. This is a rapidly growing field on the educational scene.

Do You Have Requisite Special Skills? Whereas working with people is required of all school personnel, the supervisor should be especially concerned with working constructively with teachers. The supervisor should have the ability to work with the teacher in his classroom on a cooperative basis in order to assist the teacher in doing a better job. Some teachers tend to resent this kind of operation. Others ignore it. Many appreciate it. On the basis of your own experience, would you agree that teachers are not necessarily the easiest group in the world with which to work? To be successful, the supervisor must be able to work with teachers.

Most supervisors are expected to be two-way specialists. They are considered specialists in content areas and specialists in methodology. You can see that this is a challenging assignment. A person who has hopes ultimately of entering the supervisory field must be willing to accept this dual respon-

106

What
Are Some
Decisions
for the
Teacher?

sibility of developing proficiency in some or all content areas, depending upon the level of operation, and also of developing proficiency in the methodology of teaching.

Do You Have Requisite Special Interests? A prime requirement for the supervisor is that he be interested in improving instruction. This is a somewhat abstract goal and yet a very important one. Along with this the supervisor must be interested in working on long-range objectives. A supervisor is not likely to see day-to-day improvement on the part of students as a result of his own efforts. This means that he is denied a type of satisfaction which comes to the classroom teacher. The special interest of the supervisor would be in the desire to improve instruction, and this should be accompanied by a willingness to accept long-range goals rather than immediate goals in his own operations.

Other areas

In addition to administration and supervision, a variety of other areas are available to teachers who are interested in them. Some illustrations would be work with the mentally retarded, with the blind, the deaf, the physically handicapped, and others. One rapidly growing field is that of attendance officer or visiting teacher. Most large school systems now employ a considerable number of counselors at elementary and secondary levels: it is increasingly common to find social workers and psychologists on school staffs. Others could be added to the list. If you are particularly interested in any of these as a long-term professional goal, you should start now to build up a background in the area of special interest. Certainly you should make every effort to find out all you can about the field before you get very far along in your professional training.

TO CONTINUE IN SCHOOL OR NOT

You might feel that your present goal is simply to complete your current degree program. However, if you will be perfectly honest with yourself, you are likely already to be thinking about graduate work which you hope will lie ahead. Consequently, it is not too early for you to begin considering the question of where to terminate your formal education.

Many schools require some pattern of continuation

School administrators have long realized the importance of continuing education on the part of teachers. Consequently, in some areas certification is tied in with continuing education requirements. For example, a person may be required to attend summer school at stated intervals in order to continue as a certified teacher.

Also, salary increments are frequently based in part upon continuation of education. Sometimes this takes the form of advanced degrees. Sometimes it takes the form of simply earning a certain number of graduate hours in a stipulated period of time. Also related to continuation is eligibility for professional advancement. Many school districts require that a person hold an advanced professional degree in order to become eligible for such positions as principal, supervisor, or superintendent.

Some require master's degree for full certification

It has been mentioned earlier that in some states a teacher is considered to be probationary until he has earned a Master's degree. Upon receipt of this degree he is given his permanent teacher's certificate. In these areas, in effect, a teacher is not considered to be fully certified until he has a Master's degree.

Many schools give financial assistance for continuation

Because of their desire to see teachers continue their professional training, some school districts find ways of giving financial assistance. This might take the form of released time. For example, a teacher who is employed on a twelve-months basis might be permitted to continue on his job while attending summer school. For others, it can take the form of payment of fees. For example, it is not unusual for a school board to pay the fees involved in offering a university extension class

108

What
Are Some
Decisions
for the
Teacher?

for the teachers in their own district. This is a form of financial assistance for continuing education. Also, many school districts grant sabbatical leaves for teachers who wish to study full-time for advanced degrees. This means that the teacher can devote all of his time to his studies while drawing all or part of his regular salary.

And if you do not continue?

At the cost of sounding a bit negative on the matter, let us consider for a moment what lies ahead for the teacher who refuses to continue in school. Very likely he will miss out on promotional opportunities. Obsolescence in a teacher is a real danger. Children change. Schools change. Content changes. Methods change. A teacher who does not give himself an opportunity to keep abreast of such changes is almost sure to become an out-of-date teacher in short order. This results in reduced effectiveness.

QUESTIONS AND ACTIVITIES

1. As a prospective teacher, what is your grade level or subject area of interest? Upon what basis did you select it?
2. Did you ever have a high school teacher who, in your opinion, would have been more effective as an elementary school teacher? Or an elementary school teacher who would have been more effective in high school? What made you think so?
3. What are the employment opportunities in your community for teachers at the adult education level?
4. Some teachers look upon a transfer to an administrative assignment as a promotion; others do not. How do you feel about it?
5. What types of employment opportunities does your community have for workers in special education (*i.e.*, physically handicapped, mentally retarded, etc.)?

6. Do the certification requirements of your state demand any form of continuing education for teachers?
7. Do your schools make any provision for financial assistance for teachers who are in continuing education programs?

SOME SUGGESTED READINGS

American Library Association, *Books for Leaders Who Work With Children and Youth*, Childrens' Bureau, Department of Health, Education and Welfare, Government Printing Office, 1963.

Arthur, Grace, *Tutoring as Therapy*, New York: Commonwealth Fund, 1946.

Conant, James Bryant, *The American High School Today*, New York: Mc-Graw-Hill Book Company, 1959.

Hatch, Winslow R., *Approach to Teaching*, New Dimensions in Higher Education, No. 14, Department of Health, Education and Welfare, Government Printing Office, 1966.

Josselyn, Irene M., *The Happy Child*, New York: Random House, Inc., 1955.

Mackie, Romaine P., *et al.*, *Teachers of Children Who Are Socially and Emotionally Maladjusted*, Bulletin 1957, No. 11, Department of Health, Education and Welfare, Government Printing Office, 1957.

Sharpe, D. Louise, *Why Teach?*, New York: Henry Holt and Company, Inc., 1957.

Smith, Emmitt D. (ed.), *Teacher Education and the Public Schools*, The Fortieth Yearbook of the Association for Student Teaching, Dubuque, Iowa: Wm. C. Brown Co., 1961.

6

WHAT ARE THE COMPENSATIONS FOR THE TEACHER?

Is it premature for you to be thinking in terms of career compensations? Definitely not. Presumably you are considering a variety of career possibilities, including teaching. Each of these has its own unique requirements, and each has its own way of "paying off." Information regarding compensations is important to you in the processes of evaluation and, ultimately, of decision. Hence in this chapter we shall consider some of the compensations that one could logically anticipate in a teaching career.

SOME PERSONAL ASPECTS

In our examination of teacher compensations, we shall survey them in the general categories of personal and professional. These are not mutually exclusive, since professional achievement can be a source of tremendous personal satisfaction. Some of the topics considered here could logically be included in both lists, that is, they are both personal and professional.

Monetary

In view of the widespread publicity about inadequate teacher salaries, it may seem strange that we list money as a factor of personal compensation. You might have assumed that the lack of money would be listed as a negative compensation.

The Situation Is Improving. Teachers never get as much money as they want. Who does? Furthermore, the publicity mentioned above has doubtless been effective in promoting salary increments.

Salary data are usually out of date by the time they are published. However, certain trends are discernible. For example, in the interval between World War II and 1962, according to NEA publications, the average salary rose from about $2,000 per year to almost $6,000 per year. This represents an increase of about 200 per cent. This, of course, was not clear gain, since living costs rose steadily during this period. However, when viewed in terms of purchasing power rather than in dollars, it represented a gain of about 80 per cent. One writer in this field has pointed out that: "Though the salaries of teachers have been low in the past, and still are

112

What
Are the
Compensations
for the
Teacher?

not fully commensurate with the responsibilities of the profession and the preparation required, they are rising rapidly. A teacher cannot expect to become wealthy on his salary, but he has good reason to look forward to a satisfying career without facing economic hardship."*

Numerous organizations at the state and national levels keep the salary situation under continuous study. People in positions of educational leadership are acutely conscious of the close relationship between teacher salaries and the effectiveness of teacher recruitment. Hence there is every likelihood that our salary position will continue to improve.

Increments Are Usually Forthcoming. A teacher who is looking for a better income can use any of several methods. One widely used system is simply to leave the teaching field and more lucrative line of work. Another is to work into administration, counseling, or some other assignment of this nature. Still another is to move to a school that is in position to pay better salaries. In any given year, some schools will be paying two or three times as much as others for the same type of service.

However, many school systems operate under salary schedules that provide for automatic increments. While the formulas vary widely, these increases are commonly based upon years experience, amount of graduate study, and similar factors.

Several years ago the NEA set up a salary schedule to be used as a fairly long-range goal. Under this plan, salaries would be graduated from $6,000 to $15,000 per year. Along with experience, the following educational levels were used in establishing proposed salaries: Bachelor's degree, Master's degree, Master's degree plus one year, and Doctor's degree.

Do the schools in your community provide for automatic salary increases for teachers? If so, how are these increases determined?

You Can Be Reasonably Sure of Getting Paid. We can sympathize with the venerable Ezekiel Cheever, who, after a lifetime of faithful service, still had to write to the city fathers in Boston to point out that his salary was long overdue. How-

* Paul Woodring, *Introduction to American Education* (New York: Harcourt, Brace & World, Inc., 1965), page 100.

113

What
Are the
Compensations
for the
Teacher?

ever, we do not have to go back to the colonial period to find this situation. During the depression period in the 1930s, many teachers found that their school districts were unable to pay salaries on schedule.

Financial instability was inherent in the situation where total school support came from a local district. However, in many states, larger governmental units have become more active in underwriting school costs. In many parts of America, support from the state level has been made available at least to the extent of guaranteeing a minimum salary for teachers. This results in an educational partnership which encourages the local area to be active in school matters but still undergirds the financial structure with state assistance.

As a result of the broad-base support of schools, the modern-day teacher is not likely to face Cheever's dilemma. We can usually assume that we will be paid on schedule.

What about the Summer Months? Despite the editorials that have been written about the inefficiency of the nine-month school year, this is still the standard term in America. Hence the classroom teacher is usually confronted with three months of unemployment each year.

In the monetary sense, the summer months constitute a real problem. Some districts try to help by paying teachers in ten or twelve installments, but this does not affect the basic fact that teaching is usually a nine-months-per-year job.

Some teachers have traditionally used the summer months to continue their education. In a limited number of areas, such as science and mathematics, it has been possible for some teachers to receive stipends for school attendance through institutes or special programs. However, practically any teacher whose school grants salary increments for advanced study would find summer school attendance to be profitable, both financially and professionally.

Some school systems operate a summer program which offers employment to part of their teaching staff. However, in many cases, summer attendance is limited to repeaters or to others with specific academic problems, so that few summer teachers are needed. In recent years we have seen considerable expansion in summer programs, especially at lower elementary and preschool levels.

114

What
Are the
Compensations
for the
Teacher?

Another possibility for summer income is in tutoring. Many students need extra work in certain specialized areas, and the summer months are ideal for this purpose. Teachers who, for example, have a special proficiency in reading, mathematics, speech correction, and other such areas frequently find that there is a great demand for their services. It is entirely ethical for the teacher to charge a reasonable fee for this type of instruction.

In some communities certain civic clubs make an effort to locate summer employment for teachers. The degree of success of such "hire a teacher" drives varies widely from one community to another.

Among the teachers you know, how do most of them spend their summers?

There Are Usually Employee Benefits. Many school districts supplement teacher's salaries with a fairly comprehensive group of employee benefits. While such benefits vary widely from one school system to another, certain types are widely used.

Educational leaves are fairly common. Under such a program, a teacher who has had a prescribed number of years of service can apply for leave in order to further his education. Some plans provide for full-pay leaves, while others pay a fractional part of the salary.

Sick leave is another such benefit. This provides that, during periods of illness, a teacher's pay is continued for a prescribed period of time. Along with this, there is usually provision for military leave, leave without pay, maternity leave, and others.

Another employee benefit is that of the retirement program. Many school systems operate their own retirement plans, while others use a system that is affiliated with Social Security. A typical retirement system might base retirement income upon years of service and income level at the time of retirement. A by-product of such retirement plans is that there is usually a mandatory retirement age. Ezekiel Cheever, who was still actively teaching at the age of 90, would have been retired at 65 to 70 years of age in the modern school system.

Schedule

If you were to listen to some teachers as they discuss their daily schedules, you would assume that these schedules were

115

What
Are the
Compensations
for the
Teacher?

based upon penal servitude. Yet the very features some teachers consider undesirable are highly satisfactory to others. Indeed, some teachers consider their work schedules to be part of the compensation for teachers.

There Is Built-in Flexibility. In a vast majority of work areas, there is reference to the eight-hour day or the forty-hour week. Yet many teachers are at school from about nine until three. When you examine this in the light of the five-day week, you can see that the *apparent* work schedule of the teacher is relatively light. Of course there are innumerable tasks to be performed before or after school hours—planning, preparing, grading, and others. However, many of these activities can be carried out at home. The point is that, despite the exacting demands of the teaching profession, there is more flexibility in the daily schedule than would be the case in many other types of work.

Another aspect of flexibility is the long-range, as compared to daily, schedule. The very feature mentioned earlier as a monetary problem—that is, the nine-month term—is highly desirable to some teachers. Many see the summer period as ideal for rest and recreation, hobbies, travel, and other such activities. Indeed, there are those teachers who would object strongly if they were required to extend their school year beyond the present length.

Additionally, the holidays that are observed during the school year are looked upon with envy by certain nonteachers. In addition to an earned vacation, industrial workers usually get around six holidays per year, whereas the average teacher gets more time than that for just the Christmas holiday.

Another bit of flexibility in the teacher's schedule comes through attendance at professional meetings. Many school systems provide released time for faculty meetings within the school or the system. Frequently schools close to permit teachers to attend state conventions. Also, many administrators encourage teachers to attend regional and national meetings of a professional nature, with a substitute teacher taking over for the interim. This, too, contributes a degree of flexibility to the teacher's work schedule.

There Is Constant Change. The story is told of the assembly-line worker who spent many years on the simple task of tightening a certain screw. Many chemical technicians analyze for

116

What
Are the
Compensations
for the
Teacher?

certain elements over and over. And some typists experience change only as they remove a completed page and insert a blank one.

Can you imagine a teacher whose work did not undergo constant change? It is true that one occasionally encounters a teacher who earnestly resists change, but such efforts are usually unavailing. A secondary teacher gets an entirely new group at the end of each period, and this calls for new approaches. An elementary teacher deals with fewer students during the day, but the nature of the material being taught changes frequently. Content never stabilizes. Teaching methods that work with one group or in one subject area might be entirely inappropriate in a different setting.

Overall, the teaching schedule is devised so that a teacher has little opportunity to "become stale" simply because the nature of his work undergoes constant change. Many people consider this to be one of the major rewards of the teaching profession.

Teaching Fits Well with Other Roles. Did you know that, in earlier years, some school boards refused to hire married women? In 1940 a particular high school with sixty teachers had on the faculty nine men and fifty-one women. Of the latter group, one was married. A look around nearly any school today will convince you that this situation has changed drastically. In fact, many schools depend very largely upon the housewife-mother-teacher to fill teaching positions.

One of the big factors attracting the housewife into teaching is the schedule. A mother can leave home for school as her children leave. She completes her at-school duties at the same time or shortly after her children complete theirs. Her summer months are free, just as is the case with children. Consequently, the mother who desires to work outside the home frequently enters teaching because it combines with her home responsibility more easily than would most other types of work.

This particular feature of teaching has somewhat less appeal to men. However, those men who, through choice or necessity, operate businesses in addition to teaching find the teaching schedule highly desirable. The good and bad features of such "moonlighting" are not under discussion at this point. It is simply a fact that many teachers engage in such practice.

Teaching Offers Opportunity ~~to Develop Interests.~~ Many teachers are people of high ability who could have been successful in a variety of ways. The teaching schedule is such as to offer people a chance to follow up other interests. Consider, for example, the English teacher who has real talent as a writer. During the school year she compiles a list of topics for future articles or short stories. In the summer months, she has time to develop and write up this material. She usually produces several marketable pieces during a summer vacation. A science teacher is very interested in applied research. For years he has spent his summers working for a large company in their process improvement division. This list could be continued almost indefinitely.

You will note that these teachers do not look upon summers as a period of unemployment where they must "scrounge" some sort of job. Rather, they see in the summer vacation an opportunity to follow up and develop professional interests.

Security

This has been described as the age of security. In making career decisions, many people are inclined to pass over promising areas in which there is an element of risk in order to settle into a line of work offering security. There was a time when teaching was a high-risk line of work in view of rapid turnover, politically motivated appointments, and other factors. However, in many modern schools, teachers now enjoy a high degree of job security.

Tenure. Many districts now operate under tenure regulations. Indeed, in some cases, teacher tenure is guaranteed by state law. The tenure provisions vary, but a fairly typical one operates this way: If a teacher is permitted to continue in a particular position for three consecutive years, he achieves tenured status. This means that he can be dismissed only under carefully prescribed conditions. Some laws set forth a sequence of steps that must be used in achieving such dismissal. You will note that the school board must "show cause," not the teacher. This pattern has added a great deal of stability to the teaching profession.

No Shortage of Raw Material. You have doubtless read of

118

What
Are the
Compensations
for the
Teacher?

the kind of disruption that results when a timber-producing community runs out of timber or a coal-mining town finds that there is no coal left to mine. Although particular communities might have to close schools because of loss of population, there is no likelihood that the schools of America are going to exhaust the supply of "raw material." Indeed, the challenge is in the opposite direction, namely, trying to find ways of coping with the vast numbers of students that are flooding the schools.

Imagine for a moment that, through some sort of miracle, the schools did reach the point of having "caught up" with the population. There would still remain such tasks as: (1) improving services, (2) trying to meet the needs of special groups such as the slow learner and the rapid learner, and (3) becoming more effective in the endless task of reeducating adults.

From the above, it is obvious that the schools of America are not likely to run out of raw material. This has a definite effect upon the job security of teachers.

No Loss of Demand for Products. What happened to horse collar factories? Or plants making Model T Ford cars? Obviously they closed permanently or changed to a new product, since there is little demand for horse collars and Model T Fords.

Conversely, one of the security guarantees for American education, hence for America's teachers, is the endless demand for educated people. People from many parts of the world cannot comprehend the intense emphasis we in this country place on education. Many families, for example, consider it a tragic event if one of their members becomes a dropout. We have come to see education as prerequisite to our own concepts of success. This is becoming even more noticeable as automation tends to displace unskilled or semiskilled workers.

At the same time that the demand for unskilled labor is decreasing, the demand for well-educated, highly skilled workers in practically all categories is increasing. As long as this trend continues, it will make a major contribution to stability for schools and teachers.

Some compensations for the teacher are personal. Some are professional, and some are both. In this section we shall give special attention to the compensations that are primarily professional.

There is challenge through diversity

Many types of work are relatively routine. In such work, one can assume that few situations will arise that will be new or challenging. Such is not the case with teaching. Indeed, it is difficult for the teacher to keep up with the changes that have specific application to his work. When we further consider that, even in a hypothetical classroom that is totally static, there would be endless challenge, we can see that no teaching job is likely to become routine or dull.

There Is a Diversity of Ability Levels. We hear and read much about ability grouping in schools. Would such grouping eliminate diversity? Obviously, we would never have a group so small or so carefully selected as to be totally homogeneous.

But let us consider a classroom in which there is no effort at grouping according to ability (this is still common practice). Under such circumstances, all ordinary levels of ability will be represented. Here the teacher is obligated to challenge the rapid learner, work closely and carefully with the slow learner, and give major attention to the needs of the in-between group. When we add to this the fact that each student in each group has his own unique needs to be met, we can see that the teacher's day is filled with diversity! From your own elementary or secondary school career, do you recall situations in which such diversity created problems for the teacher?

There Is a Diversity of Backgrounds. One of the most challenging aspects of teaching has to do with the diversity of home and community backgrounds of students. We have traditionally grouped students on the basis of chronological age, primarily because it is convenient to do so. Many factors conspire to create challenges out of such a situation. One stu-

120

What
Are the
Compensations
for the
Teacher?

dent comes from a home in which a great deal of reading is done; another comes from a home in which watching television is the accepted leisure activity. In one family, both parents work; in another, only one parent works; in yet another, neither parent is employed. Such differences have major impact on the work of the teacher.

We hear a great deal about slum children or the "culturally deprived" category. These, of course, represent extreme cases. However, even in a relatively affluent neighborhood, teachers encounter widely diverse home backgrounds which influence the effectiveness of teaching.

There Is a Diversity of Motivational Levels. Can you imagine a class in which every member works up to his ability level? In which each is fired with a zeal to achieve? Such classes would be very hard to find. Further, some students are highly motivated in certain subject areas but are very casual about others. A special concern of many teachers is the underachiever—the student who obviously has ability but who is satisfied with mediocre achievement. One of the most challenging aspects of teaching is the task of coping with a wide range of motivational levels.

There Is Endless Diversity of Personalities. In your own circle of associates, you can readily identify certain personality types—the "take charge" type, the type that resents direction, the quiet, introverted type, and others. All of these are represented in a class, even at the first grade level. A prospective elementary teacher recently observed a third grade class. She commented that some students always raised their hands but did not know the answer; others never volunteered but knew the answer when called upon. Many in-between types could have been recognized. One important task of the teacher as she works with a new group is to learn to know the individuals as people. And regardless of the "homogeneity" of the group in terms of ability or other criteria, they are likely to be highly diverse as to personality.

There Is Wide Diversity of Goals. From kindergarten through senior high school, youngsters have plans of a vocational nature. These change frequently, and some are unrealistic. Consider, for example, the youngster who has trouble with elementary mathematics but who is determined to be a nuclear physicist. Or the girl of very limited talent who plans

121

What
Are the
Compensations
for the
Teacher?

a career in grand opera. On the other hand, others make an early choice that is realistic. The role of the teacher in such matters is still a subject of debate. However, the point here is that the diverse nature of vocational goals of students adds to the challenge facing the teacher as she works with students.

In your opinion, should a teacher tell a student that his vocational choice is beyond his level of achievement? Specifically, what *is* the responsibility of the teacher in such situations?

There Is Endless Change in Course Content. The challenges mentioned above center around the people involved in teaching. However, the constant change in course content presents another type of challenge for the teacher. The stereotype—probably fictitious—of the college professor lecturing from the same set of notes for twenty years could not exist in the elementary or secondary school. Even teachers who are inclined to resist change have to accept the fact that, with each new textbook adoption, they must accept new content.

Many times course content changes gradually. However, many curricula in recent years have undergone drastic changes in short periods. Reference is frequently made to "new mathematics," "new physics," and others. Such changes have made great demands on in-service teachers. It has been truly challenging!

There Is Constant Change in Methodology. Many teaching methods have been with us for a long time, simply because they were and are effective. However, you do not have to go back very far in educational history to find teaching methods that have been superseded. Cases in point are oral spelling, stand-and-read-a-paragraph in reading class, and fancy loop-the-loops in writing. There is little reason to assume that methods in current usage will not be adapted or superseded in the years ahead. One of the great challenges of the professional teacher is that of keeping abreast of the latest developments in methodology as they affect his own work.

It is good to be a part of a growing profession

Do you recall that, in one of the Sherlock Holmes cases, a man was employed to copy an encyclopedia in longhand? While the monetary reward was adequate, the reward of

122

What
Are the
Compensations
for the
Teacher?

personal satisfaction would be totally lacking in such an assignment. Probably teaching would be at the opposite pole—somewhat deficient in salary but highly rewarding in a professional sense.

In teaching, many innovations originate with the classroom teacher. Most supervisory and administrative personnel encourage teachers to look for new and better ways. Rewards in the form of professional recognition usually accompany such pioneering efforts. So, a few years hence, supposing that you have by then assumed the role of teacher, you will owe it to yourself and to your work to seek out improved ways of achieving your teaching goals. The search for worthwhile innovations is characteristic of a growing profession, be it teaching or some other work.

While there is no substitute for the imaginative teacher in promoting the growth of our profession, we are not totally dependent upon him. Many professional organizations, sponsored laboratories, and other such agencies assist in this type of growth. Research in teaching is a process that never ceases. One of the compensations you will enjoy as a teacher is that you will be identified with an area that devotes much effort and energy to the search for better ways.

Another aspect of our growing profession is the high degree of unity among teachers. We are sometimes accused—in the negative sense—of "talking shop." However, exactly these same practices could be considered as manifestations of professional unity. There are many organizations available to teachers—local, regional, national. However, it would be an oversimplification to see unity only in terms of organizations. Two teachers, though they may be total strangers, are seldom at a loss for conversation topics. Each sees in the other a colleague who is interested and interesting. This is essentially another aspect of professional unity between colleagues.

One might question the advantages of being in a growing profession unless it contributed to growth of the individual worker. Opportunities for individual progress abound in the teaching profession.

One growth opportunity, of course, lies in the direction of new assignments, such as administration or supervision. However, there are others. For example, there is the opportunity

123

What
Are the
Compensations
for the
Teacher?

to serve in leadership roles in professional organizations. Many teachers find this type of activity to be challenging and rewarding. Other professional growth opportunities are to be found in such activities as workshops, institutes, and faculty study groups.

One would hesitate to use such trite expressions as "the sky's the limit" in such applications. However, a teacher who is interested in professional growth is not likely to run out of opportunities early in his career.

There is satisfaction in working with students

Does it strike you as inconsistent that students are the source of endless problems *and* of endless satisfaction for teachers? Yet this is essentially true. Indeed, the compensations that come from working with students probably overshadow all other compensations for the effective teacher.

Teachers at the elementary and secondary levels have continuous, personal contact with students. Many students desperately need such contact. Teachers frequently have better communications with students than do parents. Indeed—and this is an awesome responsibility—it sometimes happens that a student finds in a particular teacher his only channel of communication with the adult world. This role, when properly handled, can be a most satisfying one for the teacher.

A further aspect of the situation described above is the fact that the student is undergoing rapid growth—physical, mental, emotional. This makes him highly unpredictable, which adds to the challenge. Many parents as well as some teachers, see all sorts of dire implications in these changes. Usually, however, they simply indicate growth.

Growth in self-reliance is a major task of all students, and many of them find it difficult. The type of self-reliance can range from a small child's tying his own shoe laces to a high school boy asking a girl for a date. A teacher has a part in the promotion of self-reliance, and growth in this area can be most satisfying—to the student *and* the teacher.

Of course, one of the greatest rewards of the teacher in working with students lies in the area of scholarship. To challenge the superior students, to strengthen the weak students.

124

What
Are the
Compensations
for the
Teacher?

to promote effective scholarship on the part of all students—
this is considered by many teachers the ultimate in professional
reward. A student teacher at the lower elementary level once
attempted to describe this aspect of teaching to a group of
college freshmen. Finding it very difficult to verbalize, she
finally summed it up thus: "When I saw their eyes brighten
in understanding, I felt repaid for all my efforts." There is
satisfaction in doing a job well, whatever its nature. There is
a special degree of satisfaction when the task at hand is the
promotion of intellectual growth of students.

Teachers take pride in achievement of former students

The compensations that come from working with students
continue after they have moved to higher grade levels or have
graduated. One veteran teacher said he "basked in reflected
glory" as he followed the progress of his former students.
Naturally, some of them "reflect more glory" than others.
However, few of our former students achieve at such a low
level as to leave former teachers totally bereft.

It is not unusual to find former students who make an extra
effort to maintain contact with teachers through visits or correspondence. Such contacts can be a source of real pleasure
to both. And, as another teacher once remarked, "Sometimes
they remember to thank us." Even the very formal Miss Dove
as portrayed by Frances Gray Patton in her book, *Good Morning, Miss Dove*, was secretly pleased that, at the time of her
illness, she was surrounded by her former students.

QUESTIONS AND ACTIVITIES

1. Are you acquainted with the schedule of teachers' salaries
   for your school system? What provisions are made for
   salary increments?
2. Are your teachers eligible for sick leave? For sabbatical
   leave?
3. What is the mandatory retirement age for teachers in

your community? What factors determine retirement income?

4. If you were to return as a teacher to the high school from which you graduated, what would you see as the greatest professional challenge you would face?

5. Can you recall any cases in national or local history when the influence of a particular teacher was of major importance? In fiction?

6. Was your own choice of a teaching career—assuming you have made such a choice—influenced by a particular teacher? Explain.

7. To some people, the endless changes that occur in teaching constitute a challenge; to others, they are a burden. What is your attitude?

SOME SUGGESTED READINGS

Bent, Rudyard K., and Henry H. Kronenberg, *Principles of Secondary Education*, New York: McGraw-Hill Book Company, 1966.

Cubberley, Ellwood P., *Public Education in the United States*, Boston: Houghton Mifflin Company, 1934.

Cubberley, Ellwood P., *Readings in Public Education in the United States*, Boston: Houghton Mifflin Company, 1934.

Elsbree, Willard S., *The American Teacher*, New York: American Book Company, 1939.

Gould, Elizabeth P., *Ezekiel Cheever, Schoolmaster*, Boston: The Palmer Company, 1904.

Green, John A., *Fields of Teaching and Educational Services*, New York: Harper & Row, Publishers, 1966.

Hilton, James, *Goodbye, Mr. Chips*, Boston: Little, Brown and Company, 1934.

Leidecker, Kurt F., *Yankee Teacher: The Life of William Torrey Harris*, New York: Philosophical Library, 1946.

Perry, Bliss, *And Gladly Teach*, Boston: Houghton Mifflin Company, 1935.

II

TEACHING

In the introduction to Section One, it was pointed out that this book deals with the people and the processes of education—teachers and teaching. Section Two is concerned specifically with teaching.

It would be futile to attempt thorough coverage of the teaching process in this section. However, our basic goal is to give you some assistance in the matter of a career decision. Hence this section is merely an overview of those aspects of teaching that should be of interest to a person who is considering becoming a teacher.

Should you pursue a teacher education program, you will study in detail certain aspects of teaching in courses that will follow this one. Most such courses will likely be specialized. You have observed in your own school experience that teaching methods vary, depending upon the age and maturity of the class. Hence your later courses will be designed to fit the grade level or subject area of your choice.

Teaching is a complex process, and nobody ever achieves true mastery of it. However, couldn't this be said of many types of work?

7

WHAT
IS
TEACHING?

Just as it was difficult for us to define "a teacher," so is it difficult to define "teaching." However, even a casual glance at the educational literature indicates that many people have tried to arrive at a definition. A major difficulty is that each definer sees the process of teaching in the light of his own philosophy, and such philosophies vary widely. Even so, we can see certain common elements in these definitions. It is rather generally accepted that, in a teaching situation, there are those who function as teachers and there are others who function as learners. The process is essentially the interaction between these two. However, there are those who would challenge even these basic points.

TEACHING IS DIFFICULT TO DEFINE

Teaching is difficult to define precisely because it is a complex process. Oddly enough, it was easier to define teaching a hundred years ago than it is now. Do you see why?

Is it imparting information?

In the minds of many early teachers, the process of teaching did consist essentially of imparting information. An example would be the teacher in a Latin Grammar school. The goal was simple, since mastery of Latin was the prime concern. This made the teaching operation almost entirely a recurring cycle of drill, recite, drill, recite.

An examination of textbooks of the Latin Grammar era, such as Cheever's *Accidence*, supports this conclusion. Such teaching goals as understanding, analysis, or synthesis received little or no attention. The objective was chiefly one of memorization. Hence the process of teaching was limited to those steps that would promote such learning.

Does teaching deal with attitudes and understanding?

The answer is, of course, that modern education is very much concerned with such matters as attitudes, understandings, appreciations, and other such outcomes.

This expansion of goals was brought about through a gradual process. However, certain milestones are notable. For example, there was the report, issued in 1918, by the Commission on the Reorganization of Secondary Education. Out of this report were extracted the "Seven Cardinal Principles": (1) health, (2) command of fundamental processes, (3) worthy home membership, (4) vocational efficiency, (5) civic participation, (6) worthy use of leisure time, and (7) ethical character. How many of these are based upon memorization? If we could imagine a classroom in which a class was truly making progress in all aspects of education as outlined in these seven principles, what kind of teaching would be required? Or more specifically, how would this teaching differ from that in the classroom where the only goal is the acquisition of information?

Other publications in the area of educational objectives have also had impact on the process of teaching. A fairly recent one is the *Taxonomy of Educational Objectives, Handbook I: Cognitive Domain.** This publication pointed out that in the domain of "knowing," the following levels exist: knowledge, comprehension, application, analysis, synthesis, and evaluation. It is apparent that, as we progress toward the higher levels, teaching becomes much more complex.

A second volume (*Handbook II*) of the publication cited above was issued in 1964. This volume dealt with educational objectives in the affective domain (feelings). Levels considered are: receiving, responding, valuing, organization, and characterization. This taxonomy deals specifically with attitudes, feelings, and ways of responding. Obviously teaching of the type envisioned in the affective domain is even more difficult than would be the case in the cognitive domain. Can you see why the modern-day teacher might on occasion view with envy the relatively simple task of the teacher to whom the teaching of knowledge by memorization was the sole aim?

Are there other goals?

As mentioned earlier, teaching is hard to define because it is complex. Contributing to the difficulty is the fact that teach-

---

* This handbook, of which Benjamin S. Bloom served as editor, was issued by David McKay Co., Inc. (New York), in 1956.

ing changes continuously. New responsibilities, new methods, and new goals are always part of teaching. Consider, for example, the changes that must occur in teaching as a result of increasing emphasis on preschool education, adult education, education for the handicapped, and many others. The demands being made on teachers and teaching in our society seem to be endless. Yet each such demand has its effect on the very nature of teaching.

PHILOSOPHY IN TEACHING

Some people react negatively to the word "philosophy," apparently because they associate it with the legendary philosophers of earlier times. However, when we use the term in its true meaning—simply as a set of basic attitudes, beliefs, and values—we have to recognize that each of us *lives* his own philosophy.

Whose philosophy influences teaching? While we do not have a nationally prescribed educational philosophy, isn't our dream of "education for all" a basic belief? If in a certain community a school exists primarily as a sponsoring agency for athletic teams, the school reflects a community set of values —a philosophy. If a principal is committed to administration through the military approach, this aspect of his philosophy affects teaching. Then there is the philosophy of the individual teacher. Even if he tried, the classroom teacher would probably by unable to conceal his basic beliefs and values for very long. Hence we see that teaching is influenced by the philosophies held by many groups and individuals.

The philosophy of the teacher

Among all of the philosophies that bear upon the teaching operation, it is doubtful if any is more important than that of the classroom teacher. In his direction of day-to-day classroom activities, he constantly makes decisions based upon his own sense of values—his philosophy.

Indicators of the Teacher's Philosophy. There are many ways in which teaching activities reflect the teacher's philosophy. Some of these are reviewed in the following paragraphs.

Who should be taught? It is easy to give the glib answer—
"everyone of school age should be taught." Yet some teachers
find it difficult to accept this philosophy. Some teachers who
subscribe to the "education for everyone" goal in discussion
actually apply a somewhat different philosophy in their teaching. For example, Miss A, a teacher of languages at the secondary level, was basically interested only in unusually able
students. Since her courses were not required, she applied a
screening process during registration. Then during the early
days of a term, she gave very heavy homework assignments
to discourage average or slow students. As a result of these
tactics, her classes were small and her students were of high
ability. On the other hand, Miss B, a fifth-grade teacher, was
very much inclined to leave the strong or average student to
his own devices while she concentrated a large part of her time
and effort on the weaker student. If called upon to do so,
both Miss A and Miss B would give lip service to the "education for all" goal. Yet each, in her classroom, actually violated
this goal.

Why do we teach? Again, the philosophy of the teacher is
demonstrated in a question. Did you ever have a teacher whose
sole interest was teaching for mastery of content? Or for "life
adjustment?" Or to develop leadership? In another direction,
some teachers feel that it is heresy to see something good in
certain types of idealogies. Others love to get a class discussion
going on highly controversial subjects. Some worship the
status quo; others go overboard in challenging it. In our society,
we do not have an officially established point of view which
we must support. Hence, each teacher has a degree of freedom
in dealing with the question of the basic role of teaching—
the question of why we teach. His answer is very likely to
reflect his own philosophy.

What do we teach? We usually use textbooks, and many
schools provide syllabi. These as well as other guides are available to help answer the question. However, suppose that, near
the end of the term, you find that you will have time to cover
only one of several possible subject areas. Wouldn't your
choice of a topic likely conform to your own set of values?
Miss C, a fourth grade teacher, does not like mathematics.
On those occasions when the daily schedule is disrupted by

a field trip or a school program, it is invariably the mathematics period that is sacrificed. Miss D, a secondary school English teacher, is supposed to teach literature and grammar. However, she can find all sorts of excuses to devote grammar time to the study of literature. There are two chemistry teachers in a particular school. One is very interested in the way chemical principles are applied in industrial processes. The other is primarily interested in the way chemical phenomena demonstrate certain basic scientific principles. Consequently, these two teachers can be teaching the same block of content but will teach it with totally different orientations—so much so that a casual observer would not know they were supposedly teaching the same material. In each of these cases, the teacher answers the question of what shall be taught on the basis of his own criteria.

How do we teach? Frequently we demonstrate our basic outlook on life by our classroom methods and procedures. Socrates did most of his teaching by using skillfully designed questions. At the other extreme is the teacher who relies largely or solely on lecture, with little regard for, or interest in, class response. One elementary school teacher insists upon a formal atmosphere, while another encourages activity. One English teacher places great emphasis on creativity of expression while another is concerned chiefly with punctuation. Such contrasts could be extended almost indefinitely. What does each of the teaching methods listed above tell us about the basic beliefs of the teacher?

How do we relate to nonstudents? While it is true that teaching is primarily a teacher-pupil operation, some phases of teaching bring us in contact with colleagues, the administration, and the community. Indeed, such contacts can be very important in the teaching process. Suppose that you are one of the several sixth grade teachers in your school. Each of you would probably have some ideas that would be of value to all—ideas that would actually help each teacher do a better job of teaching. If colleague relations are as we would desire them, all of these teachers would benefit from an exchange of views. But suppose that at the moment Miss A and Miss B are not on speaking terms. Mrs. C is openly jealous of Mrs. D because the latter has received an appointment that Mrs.

C wanted. And Mr. E is highly critical of any idea that is less than twenty years old. Does each of these attitudes tell you something about what each person is really like?

The same patterns can be observed in the teacher–principal relationship. Some teachers have wholesome professional attitudes, while others simply try to ignore all administrators, and still others automatically oppose any innovation that originates with the principal. Similarly, many teachers find that they can work constructively with parents to their mutual benefit. Others teach for many years without ever realizing that in parents they have valuable potential allies. Still others go on the defensive in any parent conference. All of these relationships are "teaching" in its broader meaning. Each teacher is very likely to make each relationship conform to his own pattern—his own set of values.

SOME BASIC PHILOSOPHIES OF EDUCATION

In the earlier pages we have seen that the way a teacher goes about his task usually reflects that teacher's basic philosophy. From this you might conclude that there are as many philosophies as there are teachers. However, philosophies are frequently grouped into families as a means of systematizing their study. In this section we shall get an overview of three basic philosophic groups. Obviously a detailed study of educational philosophy would be a major long-term process. Hence our treatment will of necessity be limited to general characteristics.

Idealism

Because Idealism is a family of beliefs rather than a single doctrine, it is somewhat difficult to define. However, some points of view commonly associated with Idealism are: (1) ideas are of ultimate importance; (2) man is basically good; (3) faith is dominant over proof; (4) there are certain truths that are immutable and eternal. It would follow that Idealists generally are committed to a firm belief in a Supreme Being.

A classic example of Idealism is that of the Colonists who settled New England. Their total dedication to a set of ideas, specifically as related to religious beliefs, enabled them to endure the hardships they encountered. Probably the ultimate Idealists were the teachers in these New England communities. Generally the teacher was a young man whose goal was to enter the ministry. He was trained from childhood in a set of beliefs, and his aim in life was to perpetuate these beliefs.

Idealism and Teaching Goals. Because of its emphasis on ideas, Idealism places great stress on verbal ability. One of the major goals of the Idealistic teacher is the development of his students' ability to read, write, and discuss ideas. This gives rise to a heavy emphasis on languages and literature. However, he is concerned that the student go beyond the point of just reading; *what* he reads is of vast importance. Thus we find that the famous *New England Primer* used even the alphabet as a vehicle for presenting highly moralistic lessons.

The Idealistic teacher would rationalize his emphasis on abstractions by noting their role in effecting mental discipline. He would thereby assume that a student who has developed skill in rigorous thinking, regardless of the type of content used in this development, could transfer his thought patterns to other, unrelated areas. Modern learning theory provides little support for this point of view.

Idealism and Teaching Methods. As you would assume from the earlier discussion, the Idealistic teacher would devote the major part of his time and effort to working in the language arts. Assuming that life's immutable truths are to be found in the printed word, he would work very earnestly to develop reading skills. He would then require that these skills be used in reading "great books."

Insofar as specific methods are concerned, this teacher would make extensive use of lecture, even with younger children. This is based upon the following reasoning: (1) I have mastered certain of society's great ideas; (2) my students have not learned these ideas; (3) I will pass along this part of their heritage by the spoken word. However, merely hearing about such ideas would not lead automatically to mastery. This gives rise to a second major method, drill. Thus, certain content would be covered over and over again. A third aspect of this methodology is that of teacher domination. There is little reason in this philosophy to encourage pupil participation in any form, since learning occurs in a teacher-pupil or textbook-pupil relationship.

You would probably look a long time in modern schools before you found a teacher who is totally committed to the philosophy of Idealism. However, it is likely that, in your own school experience, you have had teachers who subscribed to certain phases of this philosophy.

Idealism and the Student. What kind of student would result from the type of instruction associated with Idealism? We can safely assume that he would rate high in the verbal areas—reading, writing, discussing. He would probably be somewhat on the pious side, and he would love to engage in discussions of religion or literature. His skills in quantitative thinking would likely be deficient, and he would have little interest in scientific thinking, since his educational emphasis would have been more on faith than proof. In short, he would likely be something of a "bookworm." Was this frowned upon in the Latin Grammar school? Would it be in your school?

Realism

The term "realism" groups together several more specific philosophies. Hence, as was true of Idealism, Realism can best be understood if we look at certain basic beliefs. Some points of view associated with Realism are: (1) the universe has physical reality—it is not a collection of ideas; (2) man learns about his universe through his senses; (3) we learn through systematic observation and experimentation; and (4) learning should have some sort of practical application. Many of the early proponents of the philosophy of Realism were essentially scientists. Can you give an explanation for this?

Realism and Teaching Goals. A teacher who is a Realist would be far more likely to relate his teaching to the needs of his society than to the great ideas of the past. Further, he would be concerned with the specific needs of his individual students.

Realist teaching is likely to be of a practical or applied nature. The Realist would not object, for example, to teaching typing, industrial arts, or driver training. Further, if a need arose in his community for the teaching of a skill that is purely local in nature, it would not conflict with the goals of the Realist to teach such skill.

The Realist teacher has as a major aim the teaching of a way of thinking. He wants his students to be able to attack a problem logically and scientifically. His student needs to know how to draw conclusions based upon observations.

One of the most important goals of the Realist is to teach his students to be prepared to face reality, to be able to adapt to their own circumstances, and to be able to "figure their way out" when confronted with problem situations.

Realism and Teaching Methods. In view of the unique goals associated with Realism, it is to be expected that unique ways of achieving those goals are used.

One method of Realism is the outgrowth of the emphasis on learning by using the senses. A basic teaching method of Realism makes use of experiencing or sensing. This involves activity, trying things out.

A major teaching method related to this philosophy is that of problem solving. This involves more than arriving at a correct solution. This teaching method might require that a student (1) recognize a problem, (2) design a method for reaching a solution, and (3) carry out the essential steps toward a solution. Other phases might include trying out his solution as a means of testing its effectiveness and seeking ways of improving upon it. It should be noted that this is far different from merely solving verbal problems in a textbook.

A special aspect of problem solving is that which uses laboratory procedures. In this operation, observations are made under controlled conditions. Obviously this procedure is usable only under those conditions where such control is feasible. Can you list certain problem situations where such control is *not* feasible?

There is always danger in oversimplification. However, if you were to be called upon to summarize in a minimum of words the teaching method of the Realist, "problem solving" would probably be a good way to start.

Realism and the Student. What type of student would you expect to produce in a Realist classroom? He would probably be better versed in the practical arts than in the fine arts. His reading would most likely be based upon the here-and-now rather than upon the days of yore. He would have little fear of new or unfamiliar situations, since he has been conditioned to "figure his way out." He would probably demand proof in situations that arouse skepticism, that is, he would question any major dependence on "authority." And likely he would be familiar with and adjusted to his own environmental circumstances.

Pragmatism

Pragmatism as a major educational philosophy is somewhat more recent in origin than the two discussed earlier. Indeed, the people most closely associated with the rise of Pragmatism —William James and John Dewey, for example—were Americans. So, although the roots of Pragmatism may go back to the Greeks, many people consider it to be an American philosophy.

Some concepts that are frequently associated with Pragmatism are: (1) utility or usefulness is the key to an effective philosophy; (2) learning is essentially the interaction between a man and his environment; (3) "right" and "wrong" are relative rather than absolute terms; (4) education is experiencing, while mastery of content is incidental.

On each of these concepts of Pragmatism, what would be the position of the Realist? Idealist?

Pragmatism and Teaching Goals. In view of the Pragmatic emphasis on experiencing, a major goal would be to help students cope with new, unique problem situations. Note that there would be little attention to mastery of content; indeed, content is quite incidental to the Pragmatic idea of teaching. The teaching goals are flexible, varying from one student to another. The prime goal is to have the student *select* a problem situation, design a method of solving it, and carry out his solution. Note that the student in effect sets his own goal. However, in contrast to the position of the Realist, the solution is not as important as the steps by which the student arrived at the solution.

Pragmatism and Teaching Methods. Inherent in the very nature of Pragmatism is the norm that there should not be a set sequence of steps involved in teaching. After all, how could a teacher who abhors the absolute justify using set patterns or procedures?

The role of the teacher in a Pragmatic teaching situation is that of guide or counselor. There is no room for indoctrination or even for leadership. The prime teaching method is through use of the project, preferably one selected by the student. As the student develops his project, he is making decisions, he is reacting to his environment, and hence he is "learning." Special attention is given to such tasks as learning to work with other students and learning to cope with unexpected problems.

Pragmatism and the Student. You have probably related Pragmatism to the term "progressive education" by now. These terms, and this philosophy, attracted major attention a few decades ago under the leadership of John Dewey.

It is difficult to imagine a student whose educational experiences have been totally pragmatic. Presumably he would be well adjusted to his environment (including other people), he would know a great deal about how to solve problems, and he would have very little factual information. He would insist upon following up his own interests, since this has been an integral part of his school practice. He might be inclined to resent direction, since the teachers have done little to condition him in the matter of following another's leadership.

This review has been designed to depict three basic philosophic groups succinctly and clearly. Hence we have probably been guilty of oversimplification. This is always a danger in summarizing.

A point worthy of note is that one seldom encounters a person who is totally committed to a single philosophy. As you think back to teachers you have known, you can probably see some elements of each philosophy in each teacher. However, you likely would be able to classify certain teachers as being primarily devoted to one set of beliefs. Do you see any likely relationship between a person's teaching area and his philosophy?

A great many books have been written in the field of educational philosophy. Possibly you would like to do some additional reading in them. One book that has become somewhat of a classic is _Modern Philosophies and Education,_ which is the Fifty-fourth Yearbook of the National Society for the Study of Education (published in 1955).

QUESTIONS AND ACTIVITIES

1. What is your own definition of teaching?
2. What do you think is the relationship between one's philosophy of life and his philosophy of teaching? Do you feel that a teacher can successfully use principles or procedures that are contradictory to his philosophy of life?
3. Have you ever had a teacher who, in your opinion, was an Idealist? How was this philosophy reflected in his teaching?
4. Were any of your former teachers Realists? Pragmatists? Upon what basis do you so classify them?
5. Looking ahead to your own teaching career, which of the philosophies discussed in this chapter is likely to be dominant in your work? Explain.
6. Do you think an elementary or high school teacher can keep his philosophy a secret from his students? Explain.
7. Thus far in your career as a student, have you seen any pattern of philosophy related to level of teaching? For example, do you think a college teacher is more likely to be an Idealist than is an elementary school teacher?

SOME SUGGESTED READINGS

Beard, Charles A., and Mary R. Beard, _The American Spirit,_ New York: The Macmillan Company, 1942.

Beck, Robert H., Walter W. Cook, and Nolan C. Kearney, _Curriculum_ *in the Modern Elementary School*, Englewood Cliffs, N. J.: Prentice-Hall, Inc., 1960.

Conant, James Bryant, *Education and Liberty*, Cambridge: Harvard University Press, 1953.

Dewey, John, *Experience and Education*, New York: The Macmillan Company, 1938.

Durant, Will, *The Story of Philosophy*, New York: Simon and Schuster, Inc., 1953.

Kilpatrick, William Heard, *Source Book in the Philosophy of Education*, New York: The Macmillan Company, 1946.

Leonard, Edith M.; D. D. Van Deman, and Lillian E. Miles, *Foundations of Learning in Childhood Education*, Columbus, Ohio: Charles E. Merrill Books, Inc., 1963.

Mead, Margaret, *A Creative Life For Your Children*, Children's Bureau Headliner Series, Number 1, Children's Bureau, Department of Health, Education and Welfare, Government Printing Office, 1962.

Prescott, Daniel A., *The Child in the Educative Process*, New York: McGraw-Hill Book Company, 1957.

8

HOW DO WE PLAN FOR TEACHING?

Have you had the experience of watching an expert at work? A casual observer watching a master violinist perform would assume that playing a violin is easy, simply because it looks easy. The same would be true in observing a skilled craftsman, a good athlete, or an outstanding surgeon. Yet any of these tasks, in the hands of a novice, would be most difficult. There are several explanations for the fact that the same task can be easy for some and hard for others. Two of the most important are (1) the master has been well trained, and (2) he is likely to approach his assignment on the basis of good planning.

The applications of the above to teaching are obvious. Most of America's teachers are well prepared in the educational sense for their task. However, this alone is not adequate. Good teaching is closely associated with good planning. The details of planning for teaching in your own subject area will be considered in other courses. In this chapter, the broader aspects are discussed.

THE TEACHER'S BASIC TASKS IN PLANNING

The statement that "planning is essential for good teaching" is easy to accept as a generality. But what does it mean? Actually, it means very little until we examine the more specific aspects that are involved.

Diagnosing the learning situation

Planning of any sort must have a logical basis. As applied to teaching, we have to accept the fact that we work with real people who are confronted with real tasks. Would it not be logical to base our planning for teaching on information on the nature of the people? And on the nature of the task?

Identification of Pupil Needs. We have to take students where they are in schoolwork rather than where we wish they were. An elaborate plan for teaching based on a hypothetical group of students would have little value. A valid, usable plan can only grow out of a knowledge of one group and of their needs. A beginning teacher of ninth grade English opened the school year with an ambitious list of readings which she proposed to require of all her students. After a few days of work with them, she realized that many of her students had not developed the essential reading skills. In short, her plan was not realistic for her group. She could not change the group, so she altered the reading list—and worked on the development of reading skills.

To what degree can we assume that all pupils have the same basic needs? Let us consider two cases. John lives on the family farm in the Midwest. He attends a fairly small high school. There is no spare-time problem because of the endless tasks associated with farm operation. He has never considered any type of career other than to take over the farm. Tim, on the other hand, is a product of a slum district. His verbal skills are poorly developed, and he has little interest in improving them. He has a great deal of leisure time—more than he needs or wants. He goes to a very large school. Career plans get little attention and are unrealistic. To what degree do these boys have the same needs? The answer is obvious.

Educational literature makes frequent reference to the principle that learning experiences must or should relate to pupil needs. Obviously, then, a teacher cannot do very effective planning until he knows the needs of his pupils.

Methods of Discovering Pupil Needs. Many pupil problems are so obvious they are apparent almost immediately. This would include such things as physical defects. Indeed, one of the vital phases in the discovery of pupil needs is *observation.* A teacher soon becomes aware, for example, that Mary is very popular with her peer group while Sally is avoided by them. The class show-off loses little time in establishing his identity. Those who are unusually rapid or unusually slow in learning are easily located. Then, over a period of time, the observant teacher begins to see all sorts of special, individual needs on the part of his pupils. In his planning, the teacher should try to provide for meeting such needs, insofar as it is possible to do so.

Another aid in identifying pupil needs is the *cumulative record*. While practices vary widely in this respect, many schools use this procedure very effectively. As a student progresses through the grade levels, a file of material which, in the opinion of earlier teachers, provides significant information about him is passed on to successive teachers. In some schools, this file contains little except grades and information based on standardized test results. However, many schools include in the file certain narrative-type information which can be highly revealing to the new teacher. The intention, of course, is to give the new teacher all of the pertinent materials so that he can become acquainted with the individual pupil in a minimum of time.

Another major aid in learning about pupil needs is *information available from teachers and administrators.* This can be most helpful. It might seem at first that this information would duplicate that which would be recorded in the cumulative record. However, many teachers will discuss a problem freely though they might feel somewhat hesitant about writing it down. Such matters as "this is what I tried" and "this is how it worked" can best be taken up in a conference. Also, the degree of parent or administrative involvement in the problems of a student should be discussed. Incidentally, one learns quite rapidly that some colleagues are much more helpful than others in this regard. The teacher, for example, who is inclined to become emotionally involved in student problems would find it very difficult to engage in an objective discussion of such problems.

Still another source of help in discovering student needs is information about *test results.* Many schools have for years administered batteries of achievement tests annually, with "intelligence tests" being given less frequently. Sometimes this information is in the cumulative file, but frequently it is kept in the principal's office. Some educators have come to be quite critical of what they term the "overuse" of these tests. Such criticisms are valid—or invalid—only on the basis of local practices, since there is no one established way of using such tests. However, the new teacher can find much helpful information in test results. Such items as "Joey will need special help in reading" or "Mary is weak in mathematics" frequently can be extracted from test files. When properly used, this type of test information can be most helpful in locating pupil needs.

Some *special instruments* can also be helpful. For example, there are several published scales or inventories dealing with problems of children and adolescents. Interest inventories are widely used, especially in junior and senior high schools. Personality scales, sociograms, and similar devices are also available. Many of these are somewhat difficult to interpret, and the teacher needs to be quite careful in his use of them. However, in situations in which they have something to offer (sometimes even this is hard to determine), they are available for teacher use.

There are other, more specialized sources of assistance in the problem of discovering pupil needs—the school psychologist, the attendance officer, and others. However, a basic point is that nothing will replace the observations of the teacher. Most of the approaches described earlier merely help the teacher be *more* observant.

Kinds of Information Needed. In the earlier discussion of methods of identifying pupil needs, we have touched incidentally upon the important question: But what does the teacher need to know? There is little likelihood that a teacher could ever know too much about his students. On the other hand, at what point could he assume that he knows enough?

The teacher would, of course, be especially interested in the pupil's scholastic history. This would include such items as: Has he ever repeated a grade or subject? Does his cumulative file, along with standardized test results, classify him as likely to be a rapid learner? Average? Slow? Does his achievement test profile indicate subject areas that may cause trouble? In there evidence of special or unusual traits such as creativity?

Along with this, the teacher would need to know something of the pupil's personal history if such information is available. This might include such questions as: Are there indications of prolonged or recurring health problems? Does he have a history of truancy? Juvenile delinquency? Institutional treatment? Do the records indicate anything unusual about the home situation (parents divorced, for example)? Have there been referrals to welfare agencies that would indicate child neglect? Has the family moved frequently? Is there any evidence of behavioral problems, either in or out of school?

Actually, the lists of desired information could be extended.

However, our purpose is to illustrate the kind of information needed. If more is available, the teacher would be interested in it, also.

You may have noted that the emphasis in the previous discussion is on the individual student. You actually can learn little about your "class," since this is merely a convenient grouping device. Your concern is with the individuals that comprise the class.

Preparing the setting for learning

Obviously, planning cannot be based solely upon knowledge of students. The setting within which the teaching-learning process occurs is of vital importance, and planning for effective use of this setting is essential.

Many of us think of the setting for learning as being solely the classroom. Of course the classroom is the "home base," but many teachers find it possible to extend their learning laboratory far beyond the four walls of the classroom. This, too, requires careful planning.

The Environment. Would you agree with the statement that all classrooms are essentially the same? They might be approximately the same size, but there the similarities end. Let us consider the room of Miss A, who teaches third grade. The movable desks are constantly being rearranged to fit the activities of the moment. Bulletin boards are attractive and are changed frequently. From the standpoint of housekeeping, the room might look somewhat cluttered, but it is "constructive clutter." The students are busy, and there is an easy, natural communication between students and between student and teacher.

Across the hall, Miss B has another third grade class. Her desks are arranged with geometric precision, facing the teacher. The desks could just as well be attached to the floor, as they are never moved. The bulletin board carries the same display for months. There is no aquarium and no effort has been made to give the room an attractive appearance. There is no clutter. Books are in shelves, and one gets the impression that the books are good as new. Even more important, the atmosphere is formal. Students do not approach Miss B with ease or confidence, since they are uncertain of her response.

A pleasant environment is of real importance in the teaching-learning process. However, as was mentioned earlier, a vital part of this environment is the type of communication between the teacher and the students. Ways of achieving this vary, depending upon circumstances. For example, the type of teacher enthusiasm that would be valuable in a lower elementary class might be quite ineffective in high school. Also, differences between rural and urban conditions and other factors might enter into the situation.

Materials of Instruction. The early American school, as depicted in the literature, was a grim structure. The teacher-pupil relationship was formal. And the "materials of instruction" consisted of a few textbooks and the birch rod. In more recent times we have moved toward a new concept of "teaching materials," and the modern classroom is equipped with all sorts of aids to learning.

Let us consider the case of a particular high school science teacher. He frequently gets an idea for a class demonstration during the class period. Leaving his students, he rushes to the equipment room to search frantically for the needed materials. His search might continue to the end of the period. If he is able to find what he needs, the demonstration still might fail because it was performed in haste. Note that this fiasco is in no way the fault of the equipment. It is simply that the teacher is not doing an adequate job in planning the use of it.

In later courses you will likely give specific attention to the use of teaching aids in your own subject area. However, certain principles should be taken into consideration in the use of teaching aids: (1) know what materials are available; (2) know the potential of each item as an aid to teaching; and (3) be sure that the aid is where you want it when you need it. All of these are intimately related to planning.

The Want-to-Learn Atmosphere. A classroom can be well-equipped and attractive; a class can be busy and happy; a teacher can be cheerful and communicative—and still no real learning take place. There is a hard-to-define difference between mere activity and constructive activity. The teacher has to know how to make effective use of a relaxed atmosphere in order to promote learning—not just to promote relaxation.

A set of procedures to use in setting up the want-to-learn atmosphere would be meaningless. Yet it is vital that each teacher plan how she hopes to lead her class toward true learning through the effective use of classroom activities and materials.

Guiding Learning Activities. Because of its complex nature, the learning process has been the subject of intense study. Many of its aspects need further study. However, the discussion that follows is limited to those aspects of teaching that are of specific importance to the teacher in planning his work.

The Learning Cycle. Because of its complex nature, efforts to analyze the learning process have not been totally successful. However, certain phases of learning can be recognized. One such phase is that of *stimulation.* This amounts to little more than creation of a desire to learn. It is fascinating to watch a skilled teacher in this aspect of his work. Let us consider a specific case. A lower elementary grade teacher was introducing the principle of borrowing in subtraction. She started by using exercises that did not require borrowing. Then, without any advance warning, she put on the board an exercise in which borrowing was necessary. By making constructive use of the ensuing confusion—and by a bit of playacting on her part—the teacher stimulated her class into a real desire to learn. Contrast this with the situation in which the teacher simply states "Today we take up borrowing."

However, stimulation must lead logically into the actual teaching-learning process, sometimes called *assimilation.* This can be promoted in a variety of ways, some of which will be reviewed later. However, all of the techniques that can be brought into play promote the same basic goal—that of having the student actually learn the body of content under study.

Still another general aspect of the learning cycle is that of *reaction.* Suppose you were called upon to learn twenty nonsense syllables. Through proper self-discipline you could doubtless memorize, or "learn," the list. Yet you would probably emerge from this experience with a feeling of frustration because of the pointless nature of the task. Yours would probably be a totally negative reaction to this learning exercise. The reaction phase of learning could be thought of as an internalization—the process of making the newly acquired knowledge part of you, of adding it to the body of content over which you have already acquired mastery, and of having it available as needed for future use. One could always hope for a totally positive reaction to the newly assimilated knowledge, for the feeling that "I am glad I learned it." Do you think this is too much to hope for on the part of the teacher?

Initial Diffuse Effort. Learning could not be described as an efficient process, in view of the large amount of lost motion and "wheel spinning" that is involved. This is illustrated in Clarence Day's hilarious account of his first violin lesson. He said that, as a result of the first stroke by Clarence upon the new instrument, the teacher looked as though he had taken a large glass of vinegar.

In any learning situation, it is to be expected that there will be a considerable amount of initial fumbling on the part of the learner. In his planning, it is essential for the teacher to allow time for this important growth process. For example, in the previously mentioned case dealing with borrowing in subtraction, it is likely many students will get incorrect answers, and will continue to do so over a fairly extensive period of time, even though they understand the basic principles involved. This can be a period of trial for the teacher. However, the constructive approach is the only defensible one. It is the teacher's obligation to reduce the fumbling to a minimum through reteaching or by any other available means—and to be patient with those who lag behind the class.

Identification of Objectives. What could be more important to guiding learning activities than having a sense of direction? Mention has been made earlier of various lists of educational goals as developed by certain committees or commissions. These are important. However, in the teacher's day-to-day activities, such lists may seem somewhat remote. The point of emphasis here is that, in each learning experience through which the teacher leads her class, the teacher *and* the class should know what they are trying to achieve. Application of this very obvious principle would eliminate much of the "busy work" some teachers are accused of using.

Clear-cut, meaningful goals of teaching as applied to a particular body of content do not just happen. Rather, they are the end product of careful planning.

Direct Teaching. Regardless of the amount of preliminary

work the teacher does, there comes the "moment of truth" when his role is purely instructional. The type of approach he uses is determined by a variety of factors, including such considerations as the age or grade level of his students. With older students, one might comfortably equate teaching with telling and simply lecture. With other groups, directed class discussion would be used. Individual instruction is frequently essential. Special techniques such as those used in laboratory or shop are important.

There are numerous questions that arise concerning direct teaching. A case in point might be: How long could we continue a class discussion and still hold the attention of the group? How much time should we devote to these problems in view of the other things we need to be doing? Or which particular type of direct teaching would be best for this material in my class? It is probable that these and related questions will be explored in depth later in your program.

Use of Study. We frequently associate teaching with learning, especially in describing a classroom situation. However, much of what we learn is not the result of someone's teaching, but is rather, the result of our own study. This principle is of real value to a teacher. Effective use of study periods is very important.

Many people think of homework in this relationship. Homework can be very helpful, especially when there is a home environment that is conducive to good study. Again, the nature of the community is an important consideration in trying to assess the role of homework. Others associate study with the traditional school study hall. In many situations, this is merely a lark—with very little study in evidence.

However, the most effective use of study is probably that made by the teacher right in her own classroom. The long period in high school allows ample time for short study periods during class. The elementary school teacher has a great deal of latitude in her use of study periods. This serves to provide a break or change in activity, and it permits the teacher to do her own supervision, giving individual help as necessary. When properly planned so that students are working for fairly short time periods on specific assignments, the study period can be most effective as a learning activity.

Planning the year's work

It is possible—or advisable—for a teacher to try to plan the entire year's work in advance? The answer depends on what we mean by "planning." If the question implies detailed planning of activities on a day-to-day basis, the answer is no. It is impossible to anticipate in advance all the factors that will affect class progress. But if the question refers to general planning of the year's work, this is not only possible but highly desirable.

Objectives. A teacher can do a considerable amount of profitable thinking, even before the school term begins, on the simple questions: What are my goals in this course? Generally, how do I propose to go about achieving them? Consideration of these questions would probably involve a review of the previous year's work, since this provides background for future planning.

Let us consider an example of this type of planning in reference to a particular subject area. A high school chemistry teacher might deal with such questions as this: Are there any new developments in content that should be incorporated into next year's work? In methodology? In organization? Were there laboratory exercises last year that should be revised or eliminated for next year's class? Should we give more attention to scientific principles and less to applications? Or vice versa? Are there blocks of content that are too difficult for my class? Too easy? These and many other questions could be raised before the beginning of the school year. All of them would be centered around the key question mentioned above —what are my goals in this course?

Selecting Materials. Most teachers who continue on the same job for a period of years build up a good collection of teaching materials. However, the process of adding to and removing from this collection never ends. The new teacher, of course, has only such materials as the school provides, along with that which she can obtain from colleagues, the library, and other such sources.

Consequently, in planning her work for the forthcoming year, the teacher should be influenced by the availability of teaching materials. If there is not sufficient support to permit adequate treatment for a particular unit or topic, alternative plans should be made. Imagine that the previously mentioned chemistry teacher plans a year's work with major emphasis on analytical chemistry. Then he learns that his laboratory does not have the type of equipment that is essential for analytical work. Obviously, one cannot disregard the matter of availability of materials in his planning.

In some subject areas, getting the supporting materials is essentially a matter of collecting. However, in others, as in the case cited above, the materials have to be purchased. Obviously, an intelligent job of purchasing is possible only when the teacher has done enough advance planning to know what he needs.

Dividing Content into Manageable Units. In the process of planning, a high school economics teacher reviews last year's work as a point of departure. Last year his class spent six weeks on a unit covering the stock market. Now, wishing to improve his work, he considers such questions as: Was the time allocation too long? Too short? Would other units be better? How detailed can treatment be without having to spend an excessive amount of time on this unit? Are there materials or resources (guest lecturers, for example) that were overlooked? How many major economics topics can we hope to cover in the time available? This list of questions could, of course, continue almost indefinitely.

Of basic importance in any subject area is the query: How can I organize the content of my course into manageable units? Obviously, the teacher should avoid treatment that is so narrow in scope as to be fragmentary. At the same time, a topic should not be of such breadth as to bog down the class for months. A period of preplanning before the school year starts gives a good opportunity to review questions of this sort.

Reviewing Teaching Methods. As mentioned earlier, a teacher is unlikely even to try reviewing day-to-day method usage in planning. However, it is very much in order that he engage in general planning. For example, the economics teacher mentioned above has consistently taught the unit on operation of the stock market by assigning specific phases or problems to individual students, who then reported to the class. Other topics may have been treated in entirely different ways.

The teacher needs to review each topic and its treatment, the criterion being: Was my way the best way? If the answer is "no," the next question is: How could my method be improved?

One of the most dangerous attitudes teachers can take in the methodology area is that, since this method has worked well over a period of years, it will continue to work in the future. Nothing is static in the teaching process, and no method of teaching has such built-in merit that it cannot profit from a periodic critical review. This, of course, is one aspect of planning.

Reviewing One's Own Qualifications. An objective self-evaluation can be painful, but in our line of work, it is essential. You are probably aware of the changes that have occurred in elementary school mathematics, and you can readily imagine the plight of the teacher who tries to pretend these changes in content did not occur. Such a teacher is sentencing himself to immediate professional obsolescence. Similar changes are occurring in many subject areas, on both elementary and secondary levels.

What is the obligation of the teacher who discovers that he is no longer in step with developments in his field? Obviously, he has very few choices: (1) find a way to catch up, or (2) resist change and accept the fact that his effectiveness is undergoing a rapid decline. Most in-service teachers attend summer schools or institutes, take extension courses, or engage in a program of self-study to keep themselves up-to-date with changes and innovations in their teaching areas.

A major requirement for professional growth is that the teacher examine his own qualifications for his work at regular intervals. If he then discovers areas of deficiency, he is obligated to take corrective steps. This, too, is a vital part of the preplanning process.

TEACHING METHODS THAT CAN BE USED

There are probably as many teaching methods as there are teachers. Furthermore, a particular method used at one level might look quite different under different circumstances. Hence it would be impossible to arrive at a complete listing of methods. However, certain general patterns will be reviewed briefly in this section.

The unit method

Adequate definitions of the unit method are hard to come by. However, certain characteristics are readily identifiable. Usually the class work is built around general concepts or major blocks of subject-matter. Frequently, especially in the elementary grades, the usual subject-matter categories are disregarded or "merged." There is a great deal of related activity, with emphasis on committee or small-group work. The work often culminates in committee or individual reports on various aspects of the general problem, with posters, booklets, and other student-made display materials in evidence.

This somewhat informal approach to the teaching-learning situation is in keeping with the philosophy of John Dewey and others. Henry C. Morrison was a leader in the unit movement at the secondary level. The unit method of teaching was widely supported by educational leaders in the 1920s and 1930s. However, the extent of classroom usage it was given is a moot point.

The unit method in its pure form is somewhat more usable in elementary than in secondary work. Since the elementary school teacher stays with her class all day, she could lead the class in the study of a broad area of content, working in the different subject-matter phases as needed. For example, in a unit on "The Westward Movement," the class could use language arts, social studies, and, with careful planning, some science and mathematics—all in relation to the central topic. However, suppose a high school student is studying quadratic equations, oxidation-reduction equations, *Macbeth*, and a social science. How could these diverse topics be "unitized?" Actually, Morrison envisioned a unit's working *within* a subject area more than on an all-inclusive basis.

Psychologically, the unit plan is attractive. It provides for individual differences, gives an opportunity for students to work in a socialized environment, and avoids fragmentation of learning. However, some teachers see in it a great deal of wasted motion and effort, a high noise level, and a tendency to leave gaps in the educational backgrounds of individual students.

The lecture method

This method is based upon the assumption that telling is teaching. The roles of teacher and learner are well defined, with little overlapping. Historically, we cannot say who was the first "lecturer." We do know, however, that ancient civilizations made extensive use of word-of-mouth communication as a means of passing the cultural heritage to succeeding generations. Indeed, in some of these societies, such as in the Roman Empire, a great deal of emphasis was placed upon the training of orators. Also, religious instruction through the centuries has been largely a matter of lecture.

You have doubtless seen a cartoonist's version of the lecture classroom, with the unspeakably dull lecturer holding forth to a class of bored students. Yet, despite endless criticism, the lecture method can be quite effective when properly used. What does this imply? For one thing, this method must be adapted to the maturity level of the class. Can you imagine trying to lecture to small children? Attention span should be a major consideration. A few minutes of lecture, interspersed with other types of activity, can be quite effective at the junior high school level. A teacher at this level might introduce a brief lecture period by saying something like, "I would like to explain this process for a few minutes without interruption. Then we will take up your questions." Since the students know it is for a limited period, this approach is effective.

The lecture method gives the teacher an opportunity to draw upon his own background in supplementing text material. It gives the teacher a good opportunity to "translate" fairly difficult material into appropriate terms for his students. And there can be no doubt that, from the standpoint of "covering material," the lecture method is very effective. However, the lecturer who drones on endlessly, who relegates his class to the role of observers, and who talks above—or below—the level of his listeners is simply misusing the method and cannot achieve success with it.

Incidentally, does it strike you as peculiar that, in a society in which the average person spends more time listening than reading, our schools give extensive training in how to read and very little in the art of listening? Doubtless one of the big problems in the use of the lecture method is that many people are not skilled listeners.

The recitation method

Next to the lecture method, the recitation method is probably the oldest. For example, much religious teaching has made use of the catechetical, or question and answer, approach. In the colonial and early national periods of American educational history, the assign-recite-assign cycle occupied a prominent position. In fact, during this period, there was frequent reference to the students' "saying lessons" and the teachers' "hearing lessons."

The traditional form of recitation (re-citation) was essentially that of an oral examination on previously assigned material. After this examination, the student moved to new material, continued on the same assignment, or was "turned back in the book" to do further work on previously covered material. Then, having received his new task, the student proceeded largely under self-direction.

The weaknesses of this system are numerous. Note that the teacher actually did little teaching. His role was that of hearing lessons. The whole operation was textbook-dominated, with little opportunity for the student to follow up personal interests. Also, there was a tendency for the student to spend an undue amount of time memorizing isolated facts, even trivia.

You may have observed that some of the discussion of the recitation method was written in past tense. While it is true that this method has largely disappeared from the educational scene, it still has a place. For example, in helping a student master the multiplication tables in mathematics or learn to spell twenty new words in language arts, we frequently make use of techniques that are closely related to the assign-recite-assign cycle. Our criterion is very simple: If, for any situation, a method is effective, then use it. However, can you imagine a classroom in which *only* the recitation method is used?

The forum techniques

It is doubtful if any teaching method is more widely used than that of class discussion. One can hardly imagine a teaching situation or type of content to which this method could not be adapted. It gives everyone a chance to participate; it gives valuable experience in the verbal skills of speaking and listening; and it gives students an opportunity to operate at the higher intellectual levels (such as analysis and synthesis).

The teacher's role in a class discussion *looks* very simple, yet it is exceedingly challenging. The teacher serves as leader and guide without dominating. He does more raising of questions than answering. He keeps the discussion close to the central theme, seeks universal participation, and sometimes soothes ruffled feelings. He has to promote the point of view that a good discussion cannot be based upon ignorance of the subject, so that a good participant must know his background material. Overall, there is a great deal of skill involved in conducting a good classroom discussion.

Other forum type activities are panel discussions, debates, and group reports. All of these have a place in teaching. However, they are used mainly as supplementary methods to some of the more basic procedures such as the classroom discussion.

The project method

The project method of teaching evolved largely from concern over teaching students how to solve problems. Indeed, this is sometimes referred to as the project-problem method. Support for this method dates back to the time of Aristotle, yet is as modern as John Dewey.

Essentially, the project method involves confronting a student, or group of students, with a problem that has reality to him. The student is then expected to find a way of dealing with the problem, draw from a variety of sources, evaluate possible solutions, and, as an outcome, propose his solution to the problem. Frequently the culmination might be in the form of displays, charts, working models, scrapbooks, or other such material. The science fair, popular in some sections, is supposed to illustrate the project method.

You will note that the project method provides for individual interests, motivates research, develops problem-solving skills, and in a variety of other ways meets the criteria of good teaching. However, it is time-consuming. Some students simply do not respond to the problem situation, and it is very demanding on the teacher to keep in touch with a variety of group and individual projects. So we could describe this method as we could many others—good when properly used.

QUESTIONS AND ACTIVITIES

1. A parent objected to the use of cumulative folders because she said each new teacher was "brainwashed" by the opinions of prior teachers. Do you see this as a valid point?

2. Of all the teaching methods described in this chapter, which was used most in (a) your elementary classes, (b) your high school classes? Which ones are being used in your college classes?

3. As of this moment, which method or methods do you feel you will be likely to use most when you become a teacher? Why?

4. Do you see any inherent conflict between an emphasis on written lesson plans and an emphasis on the use of spontaneity in teaching? Explain.

5. Suppose you planned a year's work at a rural school, then at the last moment you were transferred to a slum school. To what degree would your plans need to be changed? Explain.

6. A sixth grade teacher looked at test results for her new class and remarked that a person whose IQ was as low as Mary's could not do sixth grade work. What weaknesses do you see in this teacher's position?

7. What would be your reaction if you found that most of the students in your new class were repeaters? How would this information affect your planning for the year?

Anderson, G. L., and A. I. Gates, "The General Nature of Learning,"
Forty-Ninth Yearbook of the National Society for the Study of Education,
Part I, Chicago: University of Chicago Press, 1950.

Bond, Guy L., and Eva Bond Wagner, *Teaching the Child To Read*, New
York: The Macmillan Company, 1950.

Department of Elementary School Principals, *Bases for Effective Learning*,
National Education Association, 1952.

Kilpatrick, William Heard, *Foundations of Method*, New York: The Macmillan Company, 1926.

Leonard, Edith M., D. D. Van Deman, and Lillian E. Miles, *Foundations
of Learning in Childhood Education*, Columbus, Ohio: Charles E. Merrill
Books, Inc., 1963.

Michaelis, John U., *Social Studies for Children in a Democracy* (4th ed.),
Englewood Cliffs, N. J.: Prentice-Hall, Inc., 1968.

Miel, Alice, and Peggy Brogan, *More Than Social Studies*, Englewood
Cliffs, N. J.: Prentice-Hall, Inc., 1957.

Prescott, Daniel A., *The Child in the Educative Process*, New York: Mc-
Graw-Hill Book Company, 1957.

Wallach, Michael A., and Nathan Kogan, *Modes of Thinking in Young
Children*, New York: Holt, Rinehart & Winston, Inc., 1965.

Witty, Paul, *Reading in Modern Education*, Boston: D. C. Heath & Company, 1949.

9

WHAT DO WE TEACH?

In the general area of teaching, we can never get very far from the fact that we teach *something*. Hence, we cannot merely consider the teaching–learning process in abstract terms. Elsewhere in this book we note that learning can occur in several ways ranging from acquisition of knowledge to evaluation in the cognitive areas. However, in all teaching we have to start with a basic body of content or with a problem that grows out of such content.

The term "curriculum" is generally used to denote "content of teaching." While many detailed definitions of "the curriculum" may be found by even a casual search of the literature, most of them come back to a primary meaning of "the course of study." The question of what we teach is a big one. However, in keeping with the pattern we have followed, we will treat it on the basis of broad concepts.

WHAT IS THE CURRICULUM?

Think about your career as a high school student for a moment. You will immediately recall some of the courses you took, the activities involved in them, and many other such items. Who decided which courses you would study? Upon what bases were these decisions made? If we equate "curriculum" with "that which we teach," then someone was making curricular decisions that had major significance in your own life.

Some history

As is true of many aspects of the educative process, the modern curriculum has developed over a period of centuries. Hence the curricula you followed in elementary and secondary school embodied ideas that date back to early civilization as well as ideas that are quite recent in origin.

Athenian. The society that existed in Athens during its "golden age" was somewhat unique, and as is generally the case, the society exerted great influence on the curriculum. In the first place, there were nearly as many slaves as freemen, so that the latter had a great deal of time for contemplation. Also, there was a large group of foreigners in Athens, and they made their own contributions, though indirectly, to educational thought.

The program of studies followed by Athenian youths began at the age of seven. They studied music, reading, writing, and arithmetic. However, the Greeks were always concerned with physical as well as intellectual development. Hence the students devoted considerable time to gymnastics. During the subsequent stage of education, lasting from puberty until age seventeen, the youths studied geography, literature, grammar and rhetoric, mathematics, instrumental music, and citizenship. During this phase, the emphasis was upon the acquisition of factual knowledge. The superior students who continued to study beyond the second phase described above would build up backgrounds of encyclopedic-type knowledge, especially in the physical and biological sciences, psychology, and philosophy. Incidentally, and despite the revolutionary ideas of Plato on the matter, Athenian education was for boys only. Girls received only a very superficial type of training, and many of them were totally uneducated.

Roman. The Romans developed their own curriculum, in keeping with their society. Their program of study was eminently practical, with emphasis on reading and writing. Much of the teaching was done at home. However, about two centuries before the beginning of the Christian era, a major shift got under way, with the Romans moving toward the Greek concept of programs of study. This resulted in a variety of changes, a very significant one being new emphasis on oratory and debate. Actually, this emphasis was logical, in view of the Roman interest in government. The Roman ideal of a government leader was a person of broad general education who was skilled in the art of oratory. In courses on the classical languages we still study some of the orations that grew out of this background.

Medieval European. It should be noted that the Athenian and Roman curricula were not designed for "all the children of all the people," since this educational dream is largely a product of modern American thinking. During the Middle Ages, no real effort was made to educate more than a small, select group of people. These were primarily boys who planned to become priests. In part, the program of studies used in the schools of medieval Europe was an outgrowth of a heritage from the Romans.

The central feature of this curriculum was the so-called seven liberal arts. These consisted of rhetoric, dialectic, grammar, music, astronomy, arithmetic, and geometry. In each case, total mastery was the goal. Incidentally, it was assumed that all knowledge was incorporated in this package of seven subject areas, so that, if a student mastered all seven, he knew all there was to know!

Early American. Since the early American leaders were primarily of British origin, the curriculum established in the colonial schools was essentially that of English schools during the same period. The American lower school concentrated on the three Rs. Oddly, little attention was given to teaching students to write. As urban centers developed, separate writing schools began to appear. Some students in regular schools attended writing schools for part of the day on a released-time basis. The predominant school at the secondary level was the Latin Grammar school, with its attention centered almost exclusively on the classical languages.

Some Early Leaders. The curriculum that we use in the modern classroom has been influenced by many societies and by countless individuals. However, some people have made such significant contributions as to merit special attention.

An important educational philosophy was that of the French writer and revolutionary, Jean Jacques Rousseau (1712–1778). Rousseau was not himself a teacher, and it is said that his own children were reared by others. However, he used his skills in communication to protest against the prevailing pattern of education in his time. Specifically, he insisted that children should be allowed to grow naturally, and that they should not be forced into adult patterns of conduct at an early age. Rousseau set forth his educational ideas in his book, *Emile*. While purely fiction, this account of the rearing and educating of a boy claims that the natural desires and wishes of a child are wholesome rather than corrupt. Indeed, Rousseau built most of the education of Emile around such impulses, using them as points of departure for the teaching of valuable lessons.

The ideas of natural teaching and the child-centered school—as well as the child-centered curriculum—grew primarily from the philosophy of Rousseau.

Another important figure in curricular development was *Johann Heinrich Pestalozzi* (1746–1827). In contrast to the system used by Rousseau, who "educated" a make-believe child, Pestalozzi assembled a group of about fifty orphans and set up a school for them on his farm. The major innovation from this school was that Pestalozzi built much of his teaching around the work that was to be done on the farm. He found that students approached academic tasks with much greater enthusiasm when such tasks were associated with a practical activity. Another contribution of Petalozzi was the idea that the truly effective teacher must feel and display a true affection for students. In view of the very formal teacher-pupil relationship in the schools of his day, Pestalozzi's theories in this regard were revolutionary.

One way in which Pestalozzi emulated Rousseau was in the use of fiction as means of presenting his ideas. *Leonard and Gertrude*, written by Pestalozzi in 1781, is still considered a classic of educational literature.

A pupil of Pestalozzi who became a major contributor to education was *Friedrich Froebel* (1782–1852). A firm believer in the value of child freedom, Froebel was probably the original proponent of the "education is life" point of view. Also, he strongly supported the Pestalozzi idea that the good teacher was a lover of children.

From Froebel's strong conviction that early childhood education was of prime importance came the first kindergarten, established by Froebel in 1837. The curriculum he used was based upon play activities, carried out under careful adult supervision. The use of simple teaching materials that could be handled by the children was something of an innovation. But Froebel's chief concern was that the teacher love children.

An American educator who made major contributions to curriculum development was *Francis W. Parker*. While he held a number of leadership positions, most of Parker's best-known work was done during the sixteen years (starting in 1883) that he served as principal of the Cook County Normal School in Chicago. Parker's chief criterion for curricular material was functionalism. His students spent far more time studying the geography of their immediate environment than they did studying faraway places. The same policy applied in other subject areas. Arts and crafts were introduced as legitimate parts of the curriculum. This method of teaching precluded the use of stern, inflexible discipline, since a certain amount of movement and disorder was essential. It has been said of Parker that he drew from the teachings of Pestalozzi, Froebel, and Herbart, synthesizing from them a type of curriculum that was truly American in orientation.

Modern concepts of the curriculum

As you can see, we have long since departed from a curriculum consisting of a book to be memorized. For one thing, we have moved to many books, and we no longer stress memorization. Furthermore, many educational leaders over a period of several centuries have emphasized that "that which we teach" goes far beyond the covers of the book and the walls of the room. As society changes, the task of the teacher changes correspondingly, with an inevitable impact on the curriculum. The result is that the modern school curriculum practically defies all efforts to set up a defensible and complete definition. Rather, we are more likely to set up lists of characteristics that seem applicable.

Let us consider some modern-day curricular concepts. (1) The curriculum merely begins with a body of content to be learned. The methods used in teaching this content, the human interactions that occur, the procedures used in evaluating the learning—these and many other factors are parts of the curriculum. Each student reacts to a given situation in his own way. Hence, if we ascribe to this broad view of the curriculum, we might have as many curricula as we have students.

(2) Another view is that, rather than being something a student learns, the curriculum is something he lives. Proponents of this point of view see the curriculum as a contrived environment, a simplified and controlled laboratory of human experience. Under this interpretation, any sort of activity which is provided under school sponsorship and which contributes to "life experience" would be a part of the curriculum.

(3) Another, and even more ambitious concept, sees the curriculum as going beyond the mere knowing or experiencing. The key idea is improvement. Thus a student might study about his community, arrive at a list of improvements needed in his community, then set about making the changes necessary to bring the needed improvements into being.

Amid all of the confusion that prevails regarding schools, students, society, and curricula, one might well wonder just what it is that schools and teachers hope to do for students. One college student, after extensive reading regarding curricula, described her own ideas about the curriculum like this: "Well, it starts with a course of study. What happens after that depends upon the book you are reading."

In your days as a high school student, did you use the term "extracurricular activities?" It is a term that is widely used to incorporate many types of school functions. Yet if we view the term "curriculum" in its broader meanings as described earlier, these activities would simply be a part of the curriculum as long as they are part of the learning opportunities provided by the school.

THE MODERN ELEMENTARY SCHOOL CURRICULUM

What do we teach in the modern elementary school? We teach so much that one wonders how a teacher can keep up with it. To observe a striking contrast, we need only to look back to the period of the three Rs. However, as complex as the modern curriculum is, we have no reason to assume that things will stabilize at this point. New proposals for curricular expansion are always with us.

The major classifications

Despite the efforts of some educators of past decades to obliterate subject matter lines and to build a curriculum solely in terms of experience, we still find that curricula are usually organized around the major subject areas. However, important changes constantly occur within these areas.

Mathematics. The mathematics curriculum in the elementary school has been subjected to a variety of influences, many of which have been mentioned. There was, for example, the memorization period, when computational skills, taught as procedures, constituted the only major goal. Later, there was the period of mental discipline. Mathematics was especially important in this movement, since level of difficulty is relatively easy to control. This was followed by the period of social utility, when an effort was made to concentrate the mathematics content on topics that would be meaningful or useful to the particular age group.

However, with Russia's launching of the Sputnik I satellite in 1957, America's program of public education was bombarded with criticism. The fields of mathematics and science received special scrutiny. As a result, various groups began to prepare revised curricula in elementary school mathematics. Some of these were: the Greater Cleveland Mathematics Program, the Stanford Project, the Madison Project, the University of Illinois Arithmetic Project, and, probably the best known of all, the School Mathematics Study Group. Many groups of this type prepared teaching materials for classroom use, primarily on an experimental basis.

As a result of the work of such groups as those described above, several changes have occurred in the elementary school mathematics program. Some of these are (1) the inclusion of more mathematical nomenclature (sets, sentences, and others); (2) more actual mathematics content, including the commutative, associative, and distributive principles; and (3) the shifting of topics to lower grade levels, on the assumption that children can progress more rapidly in mathematics than they were expected to do in some of the earlier programs.

Obviously, if new material was included, something had to be removed or deemphasized. This has resulted in a decreased amount of attention to drill on the fundamental processes and in the near-elimination of certain topics such as business arithmetic at the upper elementary level.

Science. Science as a separate area of study is a comparative newcomer to the elementary curriculum. However, in the 1930s and 1940s, science moved into a position of major importance. The prime justification, as you would surmise, is that "we live in a world of science." Hence we could not justify keeping it in a secondary role. Incidentally, the addition of science to the elementary program created real problems for many in-service teachers who lacked both interest and background. However, most of them rapidly strove to overcome their deficiencies in this area.

Various lists of goals in the teaching of elementary school science have been prepared over the years. However, most of these can be summarized in a few broadly stated aims. These might include (1) development of scientific literacy, so that one can read the newspapers and current publications intelligently; (2) development of an understanding of and appreciation for one's environment; and (3) development of an understanding of and interest in the "scientific method" as a means of solving problems.

Several groups have worked in the development of new curricular materials for elementary science, especially since 1957. Some of these are: the Elementary Science Study of Educational Services, Inc., Watertown, Massachusetts; University of Illinois Elementary School Science Project; and the Elementary School Science Project at the University of California. However, the developments in this area have not been as spectacular as have been the ones in mathematics.

The question of what shall be taught when has been especially troublesome in science. Writers and publishers of textbooks have given a great deal of attention to scope and sequence in science, but there is still no general agreement as to the appropriate science content for a particular grade level. The result is that the teacher has a considerable degree of latitude in the selection of such content. In view of the importance of the local environment in science teaching, many teachers prefer to, in effect, set their own curriculum. Many state and local curricular guides have been prepared in science. How extensively they are used is an open question.

There have been some valuable teaching opportunities in elementary school science growing out of the "science spectaculars" of recent decades. Such areas as space exploration seem to interest children greatly. In the hands of a skillful teacher, this interest can be vital in learning.

Language Arts. One of the most comprehensive curricular areas in the elementary school is language arts, which includes all of the usual types of communication. The importance of the language arts cannot be challenged, since they feature in practically all phases of human existence.

The _reading_ area has been involved in controversy for years. At regular intervals, there are reform movements based upon the assumption that methods currently in use do not work. Certainly there are always some students who are deficient in reading skills; hence the endless search for better ways is perfectly understandable.

Since reading is a complex process, there is no generally applicable approach to the teaching of it. Some methods in use are (1) the basal-reader approach, (2) the phonics approach, (3) the language-experience approach, and (4) the individualized approach. These are dealt with in detail in textbooks on the teaching of reading.

Another language art is _speaking_. While most elementary teachers do not set up a period of the day for teaching speech, they actually teach it continuously. The problems of teaching good speech vary widely. For example, if a child comes from a home where good speech is practiced, he is not likely to need a great deal of help at school. However, the opposite is, of course, true if the child has bad speech habits. Many teachers devote much time and effort to unteaching speech practices that were learned at home.

A language skill that is frequently overlooked is that of _listening_. Much of the learning we do at all levels comes as a result of the things we hear. Good listening practices cannot be assumed in any group. Many teachers find that a certain amount of direct instruction on listening skills is very helpful to students.

Some people accuse the schools of being derelict in the teaching of _handwriting._ While we seldom encounter a classroom in which there is a period devoted to "penmanship," most teachers do make continuous efforts to help students improve the quality of their writing. Incidentally, even during the days of penmanship, some students found it very difficult to write legibly.

Another important tool in language arts is _spelling._ Methods of teaching spelling have undergone constant change, and we still have not arrived at one best method. We try to use a multisensory approach—seeing, hearing, and others. But some students simply do not respond to any known system. There are those who say that part of the trouble is that words in the English language are frequently spelled one way but pronounced another. One critic has pointed out that "fish" could be spelled "ghoti." He explained that he would take the "gh" from "enough," the "o" from "women," and the "ti" from "notion." However, the awkwardness of our language cannot fully explain the difficulty many people have in spelling.

In the teaching of language arts in general, several significant changes have occurred. One of these is the unified approach, in which we make use of the close relationships that exist among the several skills described above. Since all of these skills center around the central theme of communications, it is desirable to, in effect, teach all of them at the same time. Another change is the ever-growing use of teaching materials. The textbook is still with us, but it is now just one of the many materials that are used routinely in the teaching of language arts.

Social Studies. The term "social studies" actually describes a family of subject areas. Indeed, the use of a single term to encompass this group of specialized fields is of fairly recent origin. Some of the subject-matter specialties included are history, sociology, anthropology, economics, geography, and political science. However, in the elementary curriculum, little attempt is made to maintain the identity of a subject area. Rather, each is drawn upon as it can contribute to the solution of specific problems.

The goals toward which a class works in the social studies curriculum are somewhat abstract. They might include such statements as "improving life," "understanding our national heritage," and many others. Furthermore, in social studies the goals go far beyond mere learning. Such generalized aims as the development of understanding or promoting of wholesome attitudes are important. However, there are certain skills to be developed, also. These might include such items as learning to recognize propaganda, learning to use globes and maps, or learning to work with others.

A significant long-range development in the social studies curriculum in the elementary school is the merger of the specialized subjects into a broad area. Frequently teachers make use of local social problems as a point of departure in a social studies unit. Then, by use of text and reference materials, solutions to the problems are explored. As a result of this, the social studies teacher is a major user of library and other reference sources.

Others. In addition to the major curricular classifications described earlier, the elementary school includes several others. There is, for example, health and physical education. In its earlier form, this consisted essentially of supervised play. However, the modern elementary school is concerned with all aspects of human growth and development. Hence, there has been a considerable expansion in the physical education field. Attention is given to health education. Local health problems, such as water and air pollution or the dangers of smoking, are frequently considered. Also, many teachers see playground or gymnasium activity as an important laboratory for developing human relations.

Such subjects as art and music frequently are part of the elementary school program, although the treatment of these areas varies widely. Generally, where such work is available, the emphasis is on art or music for enjoyment, with little effort toward a finished performance in either area. In music, for example, a class would sing for the pleasure of singing. They would learn about music best in a context far removed from the playing of scales. The same idea applies in art.

Some schools offer individualized instruction for certain types of students. For example, some elementary schools employ a speech therapist to work with special problems. The school nurse does some teaching of the same type. The amount of help of this sort varies widely from school to school.

Other aspects of the curriculum

In view of the way in which we now interpret the curriculum, we can no longer treat it just as a list of subjects or a body of content. As our interest in the promotion of individual growth has become accepted, we have come to see the curriculum as being more inclusive, as involving content, human relationships, and many other growth-related factors.

Working Together. The importance of a student's developing skills in working with others has long been accepted. What better place is there for learning it than at school? Of course we do not have a specific hour of the day set apart for working on this. Rather, the teacher looks for opportunities to have students work in groups. Further, the teacher observes each person as he works with others, decides what growth opportunities he needs, and tries to provide such opportunities. The elementary teacher has many ways of providing this kind of training, both in the classroom and on the playground.

Developing Independence. Some youngsters love to be dependent. Such a feeling may grow out of a home situation, or it may just be the nature of the child. However, under the broader interpretation of the curriculum, the teacher should make an honest effort to "teach" independence. The usual, and probably the best, approach is to give a student opportunities to develop independence. Frequently a bit of nudging is necessary, and encouragement is important. Whatever the techniques used, it is important that the teacher help each student develop his own ability to make decisions and to carry plans through to completion.

Developing Leadership. It is as true of a classroom as it is of any organization that certain people almost automatically assume leadership roles. Frequently the group is quite content to have it this way. However, if a few people always do the leading, the other members of the group are denied the opportunity to develop their own leadership potential. In a classroom, it is important that, at some point, each student be given a chance to grow in leadership. This can only be done in a laboratory setting. Hence, a task of the teacher is to contrive ways of having people lead. This, incidentally, is not an easy type of teaching, since many people lack the self-assurance necessary for this role and hence have to be urged into it. Frequently, leadership potential is discovered which comes as a complete surprise to all persons concerned.

THE MODERN SECONDARY
SCHOOL CURRICULUM

Originally, the secondary school curriculum was very simple. The Latin Grammar school provided courses in one or more of the classical languages, and that was about all. The academy evolved into a type of institution that gave a fairly broad course offering, and the public high school has continued the trend of curricular expansion.

Some of the functional details of the curriculum differ widely between the elementary and the secondary school. For example, high school work is measured in terms of course units. Also, such operational features as minutes per week of instruction are part of high school operations.

In some ways, it is similar to elementary curriculum

Insofar as basic structure is concerned, the high school curriculum is similar to that of the elementary school in that it builds around four or five basic content areas.

A key part of the high school curriculum is the work in English. This consists of two phases, language and literature. The standard offering is four years of English. However, in some districts, only three units are required for graduation, so that the fourth year is an elective. At the junior high school level (grades 7, 8, and 9), students take English each year.

In the social studies area, offerings are quite diverse. Fairly standard, however, are such courses as civics, world history, American history, state history, economics, sociology, geography, and American government. Some of these are usually given as half-unit courses. In many districts certain courses, notably civics and American history, are required for graduation. In the junior high school, fused courses are popular. Also, state history is frequently given at eighth grade level.

The science area has seen several changes over the decades. The two traditional sciences, chemistry and physics, are still with us. However, two fused courses of more recent origin, general science and biology, usually attract more students. A fairly common requirement for graduations is two units in science. At the junior high level, many students have, in effect, taken general science each year. However, there is a trend toward more specialized courses, such as earth science, life science, or physical science at the junior high level.

In the field of mathematics schools still offer two years of algebra and a year of geometry. However, the traditional differentiation between plane and solid geometry has practically disappeared. Also, many schools have dropped the course in trigonometry and are using a course called "advanced math-

ematics." Courses like general mathematics and business mathematics are frequently offered for students whose needs can
best be met by them. Two units of mathematics are frequently
required for graduation. At the junior high level, many changes
in content have occurred, but no clear pattern or trend is discernible. Of course in the last year in junior high school (ninth
grade) students frequently take first year algebra. Some schools
require many students to take a year of general mathematics
prior to taking algebra.

There has been renewed interest in foreign languages in
recent years. In part this probably results from a growing world
consciousness. Changes in teaching methods, including such
devices as the language laboratory, have doubtless added interest also. The teaching of foreign languages in the elementary
and junior high years has come to be fairly common practice.

Advanced Content. One basic difference between elementary and secondary curricular offerings is in the matter of difficulty. When an author is planning a textbook series for the
elementary grades, he gives a great deal of attention to the
"spiral of learning" so that there will be an expansion of concepts as one progresses up the grade scale. While the change
from elementary to secondary school constitutes a definite
break in a text sequence, still the writer of a high school text
needs to be sure that his book serves to develop concepts and
to present new material. Nothing could be more pointless than
to have a student take a high school course which merely
repeats content he studied in seventh or eight grade.

Elective Courses. Another structural difference between elementary and secondary curricula is found in the matter of
elective courses, which are available to most high school students. A large comprehensive high school might offer a hundred or more courses. Yet graduation from high school usually
requires sixteen to twenty units, depending upon how they
are defined. Also, the mechanics of scheduling limit a student
to five or six courses at a time, with many people taking
fewer. Hence, it is essential that, in a school where course
offerings are fairly extensive, a student decide which courses
he will take. Of course, there are some smaller high schools
in which this problem does not exist because of limited offerings.

Terminal and Vocational Courses. Many high schools have for years concentrated their efforts in the direction of preparing students for college—despite the fact that few of their students went to college. However, during the past several decades we have seen a shift in the direction of establishing offerings that were in keeping with student needs. Note that this constituted an expansion of function, since college preparation has continued as a goal. Some of the added courses have been specifically vocational in nature, including such offerings as home economics, agriculture, trade and industrial education, and business education. Others have been added because of student interest or because there was an obvious need. Included here are such courses as art, music, industrial arts, driver education, consumer education, and conservation. It is likely that this list will be expanded in the coming years.

Activities

When we view the curriculum in its broader meaning, we have to include certain types of activities that lie outside the program of studies. The number of opportunities along this line varies widely from one school to another. However, in most high schools a program of varsity and intramural sports is available. There will usually be a variety of civic, social, or hobby clubs. The band, chorus, or orchestra provides an outlet for musical talent. And there are always committees. Sometimes a school will be criticized because certain people think one or more of the activities is receiving undue emphasis. Certainly this can happen. However, offerings of this sort, when properly used, can make a major contribution to the "large curriculum" of a school.

CURRICULUM IMPROVEMENT—
AN ENDLESS PROCESS

Efforts to improve curricula at both elementary and secondary levels never cease. Of course, we cannot imagine a totally stable curriculum in an environment in which everything else changes. However, we cannot equate change with improvement. Many individuals and groups devote much time to the improvement of curricula.

New content

Can you imagine trying to teach physics in a modern high school using a 1930 textbook? Or teaching geography as of World War I? The basic content changes rapidly in certain subject areas, so that obsolescence is always a danger. In part this is prevented by the textbook writers and publishers who revise textbooks in order to keep them updated. Also, in recent years, some groups have received aid from the federal government and the foundations in order for these groups to work on curricular materials.

In mathematics, at both elementary and secondary levels, major changes in course content resulted from the work of the School Mathematics Study Group (SMSG). In many quarters, the SMSG materials were referred to simply as "new math." In the sciences several groups have had major impact, especially at the secondary level. Their materials include the Biological Sciences Curriculum Study (BSCS) texts, the Physical Sciences Study Committee (PSSC) physics course, CBA Chemistry, and others. Many of these groups operated on grants from the National Science Foundation.

Newer content has been developed in practically all subject areas. However, developments have not been as spectacular in most of them as they have in mathematics and science. Further, most of the other groups working upon content revision have received less liberal financial support than have those that worked in science-related subjects.

Grade placement of content

When a decision is made that a particular block of content should be taught at a certain grade level, this is a judgmental decision on the part of someone. Sometimes the decision is preceded by research, sometimes not. But in any case, there is always a chance that the topic is too easy—or too difficult —for the age group. Hence there is need for continuous re-examination of grade placement.

One change that has resulted from studies of grade placement is that many topics that were formerly taught in college are now part of high school curricula. For example, the course in advanced mathematics, commonly given for high school seniors, consists of topics which formerly were introduced as late as the junior year in college.

A similar change has occurred at the elementary level. Most students used to encounter algebra as ninth graders. Now algebra concepts are found even at the lower elementary level. The same is true of geometry. Concurrently, topics have been moved down the grade scale within the elementary school. For example, certain material that was taught to sixth graders is now taught in the fourth grade. While this has been more noticeable in some subject areas than in others, a certain amount of it has occurred in practically all areas.

Some say that decisions in the matter of grade placement of topics could be avoided if we would go to an ungraded school. Ideally, then, each person would work at his own level in each subject. While some experimentation demonstrates the merits of such a plan, the ungraded school has not been widely accepted.

Organization of content

Along with studies of what should be taught and where it should be taught, attention is being given to the way in which content should be organized. The types of "units," described elsewhere in this book, are still in use. Some teachers like to organize content around big topics, building concepts through the use of projects and related activities. Others still prefer the daily assignment. A form of organization might yield excellent results for one teacher but not for another. Hence we are not likely to see any "standard" pattern of organization in the foreseeable future.

WHO MAKES CURRICULAR DECISIONS?

In view of the complexity of curricular problems, it is just as well that the teacher has assistance in the matter. Some might think they have *too much* help; however, we can imagine the confusion that would result if each teacher had total responsibility in this regard.

In the purely legal sense, most states have vested major responsibility in the state board of education. Such factors as setting minimum requirements for high school graduation and listing courses that can be used in meeting these requirements are frequently assigned to this board. Also, defining a course in terms of minutes per week of instruction, and problems related to it, would probably be under its jurisdiction.

The local district board of education has some curricular responsibility. If school X wants to add a vocational course in office procedure or if school Y wants to try out a new method of teaching reading, local board clearance is usually essential.

Both of the boards described above operate at the policy level. However, the day-to-day administration of the school, including a great many operational details that affect curricula, is in the hands of the principal. For example, decisions on the design of facilities, the purchase of equipment, and the selection of teachers frequently originate with the principal. Hence, he is a very important person in many curricular matters.

There are certain factors that have curricular influence but which do not appear in the legal hierarchy. For example, there are college entrance requirements. Even a school whose graduates usually do not go to college cannot ignore the possibility that some will go. Hence the school will be influenced by such requirements.

Another such factor is the state or regional accrediting agency. Schools that maintain membership in such agencies must meet certain requirements, many of which have curricular impact.

Still another influence on curriculum is tradition. Suppose a certain school has for many years stressed vocational subjects. A new administrator arrives on the scene and announces that these courses are to be dropped and the whole emphasis will be on college preparatory courses. You can readily imagine the problems that would ensue.

However, regardless of all the agencies and administrators that are involved in curriculum building, the only person who knows for sure what goes on in a classroom is the teacher.

The daily decisions as to what topics will be stressed—or omitted completely—how they shall be taught, and how each individual student will be involved must be made by the teacher.

QUESTIONS AND ACTIVITIES

1. What persons or agencies set up the curriculum in your elementary school? High school?
2. How often—and by whom—are curricula reviewed in the schools of your community?
3. In the high schools of your district or state, which subjects are required? Which are electives? Who decides? What changes have been made in the past decade? Why were they made?
4. Suppose that you, as a teacher, feel that a certain curricular requirement is not realistic for your own class. What should you do about it?
5. A parent complained that her eighth grade son was being taught material which an older son studied in tenth grade. How would you answer her complaint?
6. What controls or restrictions do the schools of your community exercise over individual participation in extracurricular activities? For example, can the same student be president of three or four clubs at the same time?

SOME SUGGESTED READINGS

Beck, Robert H.; W. W. Cook, and Nolan C. Kearney, *Curriculum in the Modern Elementary School*, Englewood Cliffs, N. J.: Prentice-Hall, Inc., 1960.

Benjamin, Harold R. W., *The Saber-Tooth Curriculum*, New York: McGraw-Hill Book Company, 1939.

Bond, Guy L., and Eva Bond Wagner, *Teaching the Child to Read*, New York: The Macmillan Company, 1950.

Conant, James Bryant, and Harvard Committee, *General Education in a Free Society*, Cambridge: Harvard University Press, 1955.

DeBoer, John J., and Martha Dallman, *The Teaching of Reading*, New York: Holt, Rinehart & Winston, Inc., 1966.

Hillway, Tyrus, *Education in American Society*, Boston: Houghton Mifflin Company, 1961.

Lee, J. Murray, and Dorris May Lee, *The Child and His Curriculum*, New York: Appleton-Century-Crofts, 1950.

Lewis, June E., and Irene C. Potter, *The Teaching of Science in the Elementary School*, Englewood Cliffs, N. J.: Prentice-Hall, Inc., 1961.

Navarra, John G., and J. Zaffaroni, *Science Today for the Elementary School Teacher*, New York: Harper & Row, Publishers, 1961.

Witty, Paul A., Alma Moore Freeland, and Edith H. Grotberg, *The Teaching of Reading*, Boston: D. C. Heath & Company, 1966.

10

WHAT
ARE
THE
TOOLS
FOR
TEACHING?

The most important single "tool for teaching" is a good teacher. However, you can readily envision the problem of the teacher—any teacher—if he had to operate with nothing except the "raw material" of the process, that is, the student. It has long been recognized that teacher effectiveness is greatly improved if there is available a variety of good instructional materials.

If we were to attempt an analysis of the technical aspects of this phase of teaching, it would necessarily take a great deal of time. However, because this book is designed to survey various topics rather than to give in-depth treatment, we will limit ourselves to an overview of the tools for teaching.

BOOKS

Books have been so much a part of our educational experiences that we are inclined to take them for granted. But books were not always widely available, and in some parts of the world, they still are not. A young American teacher on a foreign assignment reported recently to one of her former professors that she sometimes had only two or three books for a class of thirty. She was now in a position to see the importance of books as teaching materials.

Textbooks

For many years teachers have depended primarily upon textbooks for reference. Indeed, some teachers have had little choice in the matter, as, in many cases, the texts were the only books available.

A Bit of History. The history of textbooks is fascinating, since texts reflect the changes in educational thought that occurred in the culture. For example, in America, the early schools used the *"hornbook,"* which really was not a book at all. It was a paddle-shaped board, with simple text material attached to it. The usual "content" was the alphabet, with some syllables and possibly one or two prayers. In order to make this instrument more durable, the printed matter was covered with transparent horn. Hence, the hornbook was practically indestructible and could serve several generations in the same family. Certainly, by modern standards, it falls far short of being an acceptable teaching aid.

Another milestone in American education was the _New England Primer_. It is believed that several million copies of this book were sold in the period from 1700 to 1850, despite the fact that schools generally were small. This volume began with the alphabet, then moved on to syllables and words. Most of the words were oriented toward religion and morality. The reading matter consisted of moral lessons, selections from the Bible, various prayers and creeds, and the sad story of John Rogers' martyrdom. Sometimes a highly moralistic catechism by John Cotton was included. Presumably the goal of the student in using this book was complete memorization.

Another important book was the famous "blue-backed speller." This book, by Noah Webster, was published in 1782 and dominated the teaching of spelling for many decades thereafter. The lists of words became steadily more formidable as the student progressed through the book, the basic classification criterion being the number of syllables. Many of the words were totally incomprehensible to the student, but this did not seem to be a consideration. Thus students learned to spell by syllables and pronounce words which meant nothing to them. In the absence of writing materials in many schools, the blue-backed speller was often used in oral spelling. Within the classroom, this gave rise to competition for "headworks," and in the community the spelling bee became a popular from of entertainment.

Another textbook series of historical importance was the _McGuffey Readers._ This series was issued prior to 1850 and enjoyed wide acceptance for many years. According to Cubberley,* it was estimated that for more than fifty years half of the children attending school learned to read from a McGuffey reader. In keeping with the times, these books included stories that were quite moralistic in tone, and had an Horatio Alger theme.

Many other well-known texts came on the scene, flourished,

---

* Ellwood P. Cubberley, _Public Education in the United States_ (Boston: Houghton Mifflin Company, 1934), p. 294.

then gradually disappeared. However, the ones cited above are considered to be among the great milestones in the history of textbooks in America.

Have you ever had an opportunity to examine a very old textbook? If so, you were probably impressed by its general character. Much of the reading matter was doubtless very dull to the age group that used it. Moral and even theological topics received much emphasis. Because of deficiencies in the printing process, typography was frequently poor, type was small and hard to read. Especially noteworthy were the illustrations. Children in pictures, for example, never really looked like children; they were miniature adults. Furthermore, the activities of children as described in such books, along with the language used by the children, must have been completely foreign to most readers.

To this it should be added that, in most classrooms, the book *was* the curriculum. In the absence of library-type materials, the book was read over and over again. So, whether the student was "saying his lessons" to the teacher or studying his lessons at his seat, he was likely to be using one single source of information—the textbook.

Progress in Textbooks. In contrast to an earlier question, have you had an opportunity to examine some relatively new textbooks? The progress made in recent years is tremendous. You will find, for example, that modern textbooks are attractive. The publishers use a great deal of color in illustrations and in general design. Such features as quality of paper and size of print receive much attention.

However, even more impressive is the content. The stories, for example, are built around activities that seem real to the age group. Children in the pictures look like children. A great deal of research goes into such matters as vocabulary and word usage to insure that the level of difficulty is appropriate. Furthermore, these books are designed to be used as texts, not just as sources of reading matter. Incidentally, many of these same features are to be found in texts in all subject areas, not just readers. A college sophomore was recently looking at some new elementary textbooks. She commented, with surprise, that even the *arithmetic* book was pretty.

Materials for use with textbooks

Whereas the earlier textbooks were thought of as separate and complete entities, many texts now produced are supported by other, or auxiliary, publications. To a considerable degree, this factor is influenced by grade level and by nature of content. However, the practice of making available a text with accompanying material is quite common, even at the college level.

Workbooks. Among the more familiar publications of the type described above is the workbook. While no individual can be said to have "discovered" the workbook, one of its earlier uses was in science courses. For many years, and extending to a few decades ago, students in high school chemistry, for example, were required to write a highly formal report on each experiment. However, certain publishers began to produce laboratory manuals that provided space for this report. Gradually, the structure changed so as to reduce the amount of writing required, and the modern version simply calls upon the student to fill in certain blanks.

Another area in which the workbook has assumed a prominent place is mathematics. Writers and publishers of elementary school mathematics books find it very difficult to include adequate drill material in the text. Hence many of them prepare a workbook to accompany the text, primarily as a means of providing additional drill exercises.

The programmed book is a special type of workbook designed to apply the psychological principle of "reinforcement," and methods of using these books in an effective way are under continuous study.

The use of workbooks to support a basic text has now become widespread among the many subject areas. Language arts, social studies, physical education, art, music, and others are now finding workbook-type material useful. They are variously titled—learning laboratories, skill books, and others. But if the book in question is designed to accompany a particular text, and if the book is considered to be "consumable," it is still a workbook.

Incidentally, there is a continuing debate over the proper role of the workbook in teaching. The conscientious teacher thinks of it as a valuable aid which relieves her of the task of preparing duplicated work sheets. On the other hand, some supervisors and administrators complain of an overdependence on the workbook. They say it becomes a busy-work book, used by some teachers to an excessive extent. This illustrates the point that has been mentioned earlier—no teaching device is so good that it cannot be misused.

Teacher's Manuals. The early "teacher's manual" was not what we would consider a teacher's manual today. It was called a "key" and was used primarily in mathematics courses. Whereas the student's textbook included answers to problems, the key went beyond this and provided a complete solution to each problem. The teacher had the only copy, and he kept it hidden away, using it surreptitiously, as needed, to help him over a rough spot.

While it is true that the modern manual is also designed for teacher usage, there is no longer anything reprehensible about owning one. Indeed, it is a potentially valuable resource. The emphasis in a good teacher's manual that accompanies a modern text is on teaching methods. Suggestions are made on ways of treating each topic. Reading lists, suggestions for class reports, and other materials of this type are included.

The teacher's manual can be of real service to the teacher, especially if he is new at the job. This manual is designed to parallel the textbook, and it is usually prepared by or in collaboration with the textbook authors.

Incidentally, some teacher's-manual-type material frequently is incorporated into the textbook itself. Some books will, in the body of the text, include "suggestions of things to do," such as simple science experiments. Others will have such material at the end of the chapter. These lists can be of real service to both student and teacher.

Reading Lists and Bibliographies. The danger of overdependence upon a single textbook can be avoided if the teacher is willing to make effective use of the work that has been done for him along this line. Nearly any major textbook will provide, within the book itself or in the accompanying teacher's manual, a list of collateral readings. These might be informal reading lists, or they could be organized into standard bibliographic form. In either case, such material simplifies the task of the teacher in assigning "outside reading" to her students.

A fairly recent development along this line is the "book of readings." Frequently in paperback form, these books include a substantial number of excerpts from the works themselves, not just lists of recommended readings by title. In a book of readings to accompany an American history course, for example, there might be found copies of the Declaration of Independence, the Constitution, Washington's Farewell address, and many other such documents. This method of providing reading material has been well received by teachers.

Recordings, Films, Filmstrips. Some work has been done in devising audiovisual aids such as recordings and films designed specifically to support particular textbooks. This is, of course, quite different from using these media in a more generalized way. An illustration of this procedure might be as follows: An author writes a textbook on the history of his state. He "supports" his text by preparing a series of filmstrips about historical sites in the state and prepares a recording to supply a commentary on the sites as they are being viewed. This approach has much potential but has not been widely adopted, probably because of the expense involved.

Supplementary books

You will note that the previous section dealt primarily with textbooks and with other materials that relate to texts. However, in the modern school, the teacher has available an extensive variety of nontext reading matter to supplement the text.

The Library. A few decades ago, many high schools had what they called a library in a corner of a classroom or study hall. Frequently, the only person in attendance was a student helper, who worked under the very casual supervision of the English teacher. Collections were woefully inadequate. Outside of some required "back reports" in their English classes, students had little use for the library, and most faculty members used it even less.

During the last several decades, however, the school library has undergone rapid growth, and there is every likelihood that this will continue. The availability of funds from federal sources has been a major stimulus in this regard. Also, the trend toward separate libraries for the elementary schools, under the direction of a trained librarian, has been a step forward.

While collections have improved, the services provided by the library have improved even more. The librarian is a valued professional colleague of the modern-day teacher. Libraries are beginning to evolve in the direction of general learning centers. Though this does not represent a downgrading of the role of books, it does indicate that other types of services are also becoming viewed as necessary. For example, in many schools the library has come to be the central depository for audiovisual equipment.

Encyclopedias and Similar Reference Works. Most of us probably use "library books" to mean the single-volume type, including such material as fiction and biography. However, the more important library holdings are the reference books, which frequently are in sets. Included are the standard encyclopedias, unabridged dictionaries, atlases, and others. Such volumes are of tremendous value to the teacher as text supplements.

In many schools, we find sets of encyclopedias in the classroom as well as in the library. While this is expensive, it does serve to increase usage of these references. Some students use books if they are immediately available but might not take the trouble to go to the library.

Newspapers, Pamphlets, Magazines. Did your social studies teacher in high school occasionally have a "current events" day? Many of them use this technique, while others try to relate current events to their historical backgrounds. Whatever the method used, it is important that students study the here and now as well as the past. However, it would be unrealistic for the teacher to assume that every student's home is supplied with newspapers and periodicals. Furthermore, he cannot assume that all students read such material at home, even if it is available. Consequently, the teacher needs to make use of such reading matter at school.

Many teachers like to supplement the library copies of current reading material by having at least a limited amount of it in their classrooms. While this may not be feasible with daily newspapers, it usually is practicable for news magazines and pamphlets. The latter, incidentally, frequently are troublesome for the librarian because they are hard to catalog and are usually of passing interest. Some teachers have observed that students make more use of classroom copies of material for browsing than they would if the only copies were located in the school library.

In summary, the textbook is still important in teaching. It is usually the one source of information that is available to every student in the class. It frequently provides the structural basis upon which a course is built. However, the modern teacher would have to undergo a drastic change in policy and procedure if he found it necessary to teach *the* book in the sense that the teachers of earlier generations did.

AUDIOVISUAL AIDS

There is still much we do not know about the learning process. However, some principles have been understood for a long time. One such is the principle that we learn better when we involve several senses. In teaching the numerals to a small child, for example, it is good to use plastic or wood models so that the youngster uses both sight and touch. Or, if only a single sense is involved, presentation of material in a variety of forms or structures helps. Thus the data from an experiment might be presented in a table as well as in a bar or circle graph.

It was from knowledge that the whole field of audiovisual instruction has developed. It is now a large, specialized area of study, an area that is undergoing constant change.

Films

Textbooks were greatly improved by the addition of pictures and other types of illustrations. However, text pictures could not portray motion effectively. So, when films became available to teachers, a whole new dimension was added to teaching materials.

Although films were and are associated with entertainment, there can be no doubt that, when properly used, they are very effective teaching aids. Some uses of films will be considered later.

Availability. The degree of availability of films varies from one school to another. However, some films are available to any teacher who will take the trouble to get them. For example, some state departments of education have extensive film libraries for school use. In some areas this is centralized, but certain states have set up regional distribution points, making it feasible for many teachers to pick up the films they need, while others order by mail.

Many local districts now have their own film collections. This practice is more common in urban centers, since films are quite expensive, and the cost of local ownership can be prohibitive for small districts. Federal funds have made it possible for many systems to set up audiovisual centers, which include films.

In addition to state and local sources, there are commercial sources of films. Many of the major producers of educational films will either sell or rent films. Hence a teacher who needs a particular film can usually obtain it by paying a nominal rental fee. Also, some large industrial concerns own films about their operations. These are usually circulated without cost to schools. An example is the excellent films about the petroleum industry that are circulated by one of the major oil companies.

Use of Films. It would be a platitude to say that we use films whenever they will help in the teaching process. Yet that is the governing principle. Some teachers find a carefully selected film is an effective way to introduce a new unit. The right film can arouse interest in the new topic while providing essential background. Other teachers prefer to use a film at the culmination of a unit. They find that the proper film will summarize a block of content more effectively and in less time than is the case with most other teaching aids.

However, one of the prime advantages of film use is that you can show effects that are not seen by any other method. The classic case is the one in which we watch a bud become a flower. This process requires many hours in actuality but can be seen in seconds or minutes on film. Again, a physics teacher had used the text, along with board diagrams and his own powers of explanation, but he felt that his class still was not clear on the complex operation of a storage cell. However, a film, making very effective use of animation, provided the additional information that was needed to clarify some troublesome points.

Any teaching device can be misused, and films are no exception. A few principles of effective use are worthy of note. (1) The teacher should be sure the film will do what he wants it to do. A film that is grossly unsuited to the age group will produce frustration—or hilarity. Also, consider the case of a geometry teacher who ordered a film on congruent triangles from the film library operated by the large school system in which he worked. When the film arrived, it was on "How to Answer the Telephone"! Obviously, the only way for the teacher to know if the film in question will function in his own class is to preview it. (2) The film should fit into the situation naturally and logically—simply as another teaching device. The teacher who, in making an assignment says, "Tomorrow we will have a movie," and lets it go at that is inviting a holiday spirit. Many teachers do not make a prior announcement in such situations. (3) Something should be expected of the student during and after the movie, otherwise it is likely he will assume the role of spectator rather than that of participant. Many teachers prior to showing a movie will list questions for which the student should try to find answers. Then the teachers follow up with a short test at the end of the showing. This type of approach tends to make the film an integral part of class activity.

Filmstrips

The filmstrip is essentially just a sequence of still pictures. However, these pictures are organized into a pattern so as to present an idea or principle in a logical order. Captions are used for explanation, although the filmstrip that is synchronized with a recording is quite popular. One might wonder why, in the absence of animation on the film, the textbook illustrations could not serve as well as the filmstrip. The main difference is that, although the student examines one picture at a time in both cases, the frames of the filmstrip are sequenced in such a way as to present an idea developmentally.

Availability. Generally the same sources that supply films also supply filmstrips. However, there are some suppliers that concentrate on filmstrips to the exclusion of films. If you have access to catalogs issued by these suppliers, you will find that there is an abundant supply of filmstrips available, and new ones are constantly being produced.

One factor that favors the filmstrip is that of low cost. Whereas the standard-length film might cost well above a hundred dollars (if in color), many filmstrips can be purchased for the same amount of money. This, of course, makes the filmstrip more readily available. As an added difference, the filmstrip projector is much less expensive than the film projector.

Use of Filmstrips. In many ways the use of filmstrips parallels that of films. However, generally the teacher has more control of the situation with filmstrips. For example, the teacher can provide his own commentary, so that the content of the filmstrip can be correlated very closely with the material under study. Also, the teacher controls the speed of coverage with the filmstrip. If a particular frame is of incidental interest, it can be dealt with briefly, and it would not be unlikely that a major part of a class period could be spent on certain key parts of the strip. Indeed, some teachers seldom show all of a filmstrip. Rather, they locate those frames that are specifically applicable to the topic under study and use them. As you can see from this discussion, the filmstrip is a very adaptable visual aid.

Recordings

We can become so conditioned to the term "audiovisual" that we overlook certain teaching materials that are either audio or visual but not both. A case in point is the tape or disk recording. The latter device has been used for many years in teaching music or drama, in various rhythm activities for small children, and in a variety of other ways. The tape recording has proved to be an extremely versatile instrument. It is, for example, a key component in the language laboratory. In speech class, students record and study their own speeches. It can be especially valuable in locating speech defects.

In some schools, the learning center keeps a file of tapes of particularly significant lectures and related materials for circulation to students. Indeed, we read a great deal about schools in which entire courses are taped, the tapes being designed for use in conjunction with certain visual materials. The experimental work along this line has been concentrated primarily in the area of higher education. However, as procedures are developed, they will doubtless have impact upon the elementary and secondary schools.

Models

Pictorial materials are frequently supplemented by models of one type or another. These can take a variety of forms.

Working Models. Many fairly complex processes can be presented with working models. Consider as an illustration the lift pump. The text might present a sequence of pictures showing the positions of the piston and the valves during each phase of operation. However, the working model, made of glass or plastic, permits the student to actually observe the motion of the piston and the opening or closing of the valves as water is being pumped. The same type of teaching materials are available in widely diverse forms and subject areas. They are most helpful when the class is studying processes or operations.

Scale Models. Despite the amount of effort put into the task by teachers, it is doubtful that the teaching of a subject such as world geography could ever be very meaningful without a globe. For many other types of situations a map is a valuable aid. In shop work, the blueprint is essential. All of these, and others that could be listed, represent the use of scale models. Of course the globe, if set in motion in the proper way, could also be thought of as a working model.

Frequently a class project can result in the production of a good scale model that is of local interest. A case in point is a relief map of the campus or of the local community, built of a plastic material. This can be of value not only to those who build it but also to subsequent classes.

Charts and photographs

The photograph has long served as a valuable teaching aid in the textbook. The addition of color has increased its effectiveness, especially in showing contrasts. This type of teaching aid has a valuable supplement in the large charts that are widely used. The illustrations are of a size such that all the members of the class can see them. This makes teaching much easier. Can you see the basic difference between this and using the same diagram from the text? Can you imagine trying to get every member of a class to see the same thing from a book diagram?

Many of us remember the chart in connection with science classes. The study of stem cross-sections, of flowers, fruits, and similar material can be greatly simplified by using chart-size illustrations. Even more valuable is the enlargement. The study of the cell or of simple plants and animals could well be adapted to this method.

Another feature of the chart is its use of sequentials. For example, in illustrating the process of fertilization in plants, a sequence of steps can be shown in such a way as to make unified treatment possible. Another form of sequential that is fairly popular is the overlay. This is sometimes used in textbooks. There is a basic diagram, with transparent overlays adjacent to it. Different systems can be added to the basic diagram by proper use of the overlays.

A variation of the chart is the microprojector. In using this device, a picture on a transparent slide is enlarged and projected so that the entire class sees the same image. The projection equipment is fairly expensive, so that this device is not likely to replace the simple chart.

Specimens

Instead of using a picture or diagram why not use the real object? This can sound very convincing, and indeed it is frequently done. However, there are certain built-in distractions in using specimens. Do you remember the squeals when certain of your classmates tried to "study" such specimens as a live snake or mouse?

One popular type of specimen is the ant colony or the beehive. These are available from commercial suppliers and can become part of the classroom. When properly used, they can be quite effective. However, they can be just as effective as distracters. Can you imagine a junior high school student giving full attention to the teacher when he *could* be watching the fascinating activity that goes on in a beehive?

For certain age groups, the dissected specimen can be a good teaching aid. In studying the systems of a frog, for example, a dissected specimen can be arranged as a good demonstration. However, some explanations and a certain amount of guidance are as essential here as would be the case in studying a diagram.

Have you ever been in an elementary classroom that looked like a branch of the local zoo? Smaller children are born collectors, and they like to share their prizes with friends. So what could be more logical than to bring any interesting insect, worm, mouse, cat, or dog to school? Frequently the interest thus generated can be used in good teaching. However, the teacher usually breathes a sigh of relief when she is able to return the live animal to its natural habitat.

OTHER TOOLS FOR TEACHING

Many good teaching tools fail to fit into the obvious categories such as books and audiovisual aids. Yet some of these are coming to occupy prominent positions in the total educative effort.

Commercial television

A teacher recently remarked that she had no doubt television teaches, since a class discussion on practically any topic involves comments of the "I saw on TV . . ." type. Furthermore, many shows can be quite educational in nature. Even the ever-present western has something to teach, especially to youngsters who live in urban areas. Also, some companies have sponsored important educational shows, usually as "specials." Included are symphonic or dramatic performances, special shows on scientific topics, panel discussions, and the all-important "current events." We are still looking for a good way to make maximum use of such educational opportunities. Some teachers assign shows to be watched at home, with a discussion in class the following day. Some actually convene the class at school and watch the show in the classroom. One teacher even engages the class in an intermittent discussion during commercials.

In some parts of the country the TV stations carry educational programs in the early morning hours. Frequently, these present distinguished lecturers, along with an extensive array of teaching aids. However, this has not become a major movement as had been hoped. Some people simply object to getting up early to watch TV. Also, we have not yet devised a system to make maximum use of the TV offering.

Educational television

When the television field was developing, the Federal Communications Commission reserved certain channels for use in educational broadcasting. Some sections of the nation have developed this type of teaching to a very high degree, while others have done little or nothing about it.

One of the big advantages of educational TV is its flexibility, in that programs can be developed to meet local needs. Also, broadcast programs are available during school hours, so that they can become an integral part of the class activity. The fact that there is usually extensive use of local talent adds appeal. The proponents point out that, by using educational TV, you can "multiply good teaching." However, the critics add that such a broadcast is often equally effective in multiplying poor teaching.

One reason for the relatively slow growth of educational TV is that of cost, of both installation and operation. Another is that despite our best efforts to the contrary, TV still places the student in the role of an observer rather than that of participant. Also, we are still looking for better ways to utilize this valuable tool.

Closed circuit television

The prime mechanical difference between closed circuit and the other types of TV is that, in the technical sense, the closed circuit program is not broadcast. Rather it is "piped in" to groups. This, of course, permits the institution to control not only program content but also program recipients.

The area of rapid growth for closed circuit TV is higher education, presumably because TV rather closely resembles the lecture-type teaching that is widely used in colleges. It is said that, in some sections where there are large numbers of of colleges and universities, as many as fifty of them may collaborate in a closed circuit network. The idea is, of course, to make maximum use of distinguished teachers, regardless of their "home base."

This tool also has a place in helping to make some types of teaching more effective. For example, in medical education, students have traditionally observed surgery by grouping around and above the surgeon, seeing as best they can. However, if the operation is televised, students can sit in auditoriums or classrooms far removed from the surgery and still see it better than if they were in the operating room.

With the rapid growth of college enrollments, ways must be found to use large-group instruction. Hence, it is becoming common practice to have a single professor lecture to hundreds, even thousands of students who are located in large lecture halls over the campus. Also, the lectures frequently are taped so that they can be reused as long as they are timely. This differs from most other types of TV in that the students are registered for the course, have assigned reading materials, take tests and examinations, and receive marks.

Computers

One hears frequent references to "computerized instruction." This generally takes the direction of having the student give answers to a computer which responds by telling the student whether he is right or wrong. Some rather sophisticated "conversation" between student and computer is possible. The factor of cost is a big drawback in the development of computerized systems. Also, instructional procedures have not been perfected. In future years this may be an area of major development.

QUESTIONS AND ACTIVITIES

1. Do you have access to any old textbooks? Many of them tell us a great deal about earlier schools. It is especially

enlightening to compare several books for students of different ages in the same subject area.

2. Have you ever had a teacher who, in your opinion, was unusually effective in the use of audiovisual aids? What techniques made this phase of his teaching unique?

3. What audiovisual equipment would you consider essential for your own classroom? Explain.

4. Have the schools of your community made use of educational TV? How has it worked out?

5. For the subject or grade level in which you propose to work, how would you use workbooks?

6. What do you see as the proper role of library materials in your teaching?

7. How could newspapers be used as teaching materials by a teacher of mathematics? Of foreign languages? Of industrial arts?

SOME SUGGESTED
READINGS

Beauchamp, George A., *Basic Dimensions of Elementary Method*, Boston: Allyn & Bacon, Inc., 1959.

Hickerson, J. Allen, *Guiding Children's Arithmetic Experiences*, Englewood Cliffs, N. J.: Prentice-Hall, Inc., 1952.

Hill, Wilhelmina, *Unit Planning and Teaching in Elementary Social Studies*, Bulletin 1963, No. 23, Department of Health, Education and Welfare, Government Printing Office, 1963.

Kilpatrick, William Heard, *The Montessori System Examined*, Boston: Houghton Mifflin Company, 1914.

Mehl, Marie A., Hubert H. Mills, and Harl R. Douglas, *Teaching in the Elementary School*, New York: The Ronald Press Company, 1950.

Shipp, Donald E., and Sam Adams, *Developing Arithmetic Concepts and Skills*, Englewood Cliffs, N. J.: Prentice-Hall, Inc., 1964.

Smith, Fred M., and Sam Adams, *Educational Measurement for the Classroom Teacher*, New York: Harper & Row, Publishers, 1966.

11

TEACHING, TESTING, EVALUATING

In our survey of teaching, it is essential that we give attention to that form of teaching called testing. Is testing teaching? Actually, testing is another method of teaching, and when properly used, it can be a very effective method.

The related term, evaluation, is somewhat different in that it supposedly indicates the outcome of the teaching-learning process. Most of us associate evaluation with the giving of grades. This process is an outgrowth of testing and other measurement procedures in combination with judgmental factors.

TESTING

A student recently remarked about a former teacher "I don't remember very much of what he taught me, but I will long remember his tests." It developed that this teacher concentrated his testing on minor points, footnotes, and items that were given very casual treatment in class. In essence, his tests were sort of like guessing games—very serious guessing games.

Achievement tests

Tests are classified in a variety of ways. One very important type is the achievement test. All teaching should be directed toward helping the student progress toward certain well-defined goals. An achievement test should serve as an indicator as to how near—or far—the student is from the goal. At the risk of oversimplification, we could say that, through an achievement test, the teacher tries to find out how much the student knows about a certain block of content.

Teacher-made Tests. Although other types of tests (to be discussed later) are used in achievement testing, the most widely used test in the achievement area is the one prepared by the teacher. This is as it should be. After all, who else is in a position to know exactly what has been taught in the classroom? While it is not feasible to go into detail here regarding the process of test-making, it should be emphasized that the making of good tests is a demanding, time-consuming process. You will probably have other courses dealing specifically with this aspect of teaching.

An important type of teacher-made test is the *short daily quiz.* Did it ever occur to you that one of the best learning experiences comes from preparing for a test? Many teachers make use of this principle by testing frequently. This test can be fitted into any part of the class period. One very good method of use is to announce at the end of today's period that our first order of business tomorrow will be a short test over material covered today. What is your opinion of the unannounced "pop quiz"? There are situations in which it doubtless serves a useful purpose. However, since preparation for a test is an important phase of study, a teacher actually forfeits good learning experience for his students if he uses extensively the unannounced test.

Then there is the major *unit test.* This, of course, covers a fairly large block of content. Hence, the test must be longer, and the time allocation for test-taking must be greater, than for the daily quiz. What you may not have realized is that the time required for test preparation on the part of the teacher is greater, also.

The major test is not widely used with small children, for obvious reasons. However, it is of real value in classes for older children. Ample time should be allowed for test preparation, so this test should be announced several days before the date of administration. Also, the results of the test should influence subsequent teaching. If there are certain phases of content that give trouble on the test, reteaching should be undertaken. You will note that, in a sense, the test serves as a communications device between teacher and students. If the test is to perform this role properly, it is important that the test accurately reflects the content as it was taught. In other words, testing emphases should closely parallel teaching emphases.

Another important teacher-made achievement test is the *examination.* We usually think of this term in association with grading periods—six weeks, nine weeks, midterm, final, etc. Generally, this test reflects all of the material covered during the period in question. Again, this is an important teaching situation in that the student, while preparing for the test, must review a large block of content. Frequently this helps him see relationships between units that have been isolated in previous treatment.

In some school systems there is a practice of exempting students from examinations—for academic reasons or even for attendance. This procedure is apparently based upon the assumption that examinations are a form of punishment; hence, some students should be spared. This position is hard to defend if we view the examination in its proper role—as a valuable educational experience. This means simply that the student being exempted is denied part of what is due him and hence is actually being penalized.

Let us now consider some of the structural aspects of teacher-made tests. From the historical point of view, the *oral test* came first. The first schools in America, borrowing from their English counterparts, made extensive use of the oral test. The weaknesses of this method were many: It was more a test of poise than of achievement, the sampling was woefully inadequate, and it was highly inefficient, requiring that several adults quiz a single student. This type of test is still used in many graduate schools. Also, some classroom teachers like to use it on occasion. Did you ever have a teacher who started the class period with a brief oral test over previous work? This can be a good way to relate the new content with the old. However, many teachers who use this technique do not try to grade students on oral performance, so that this period is more review than test.

Next in historical sequence, was the *essay test*.* This test could not, of course, be adopted for school use until students had writing materials available. For many decades, and continuing well into this century, the essay test was essentially the only one in use. However, a series of published studies began to cast doubt upon the essay test as a measuring instrument. Teachers were found to differ greatly on evaluating essay tests. Further, other studies showed that a teacher, in reevaluating the same paper after a lapse of a few weeks, might well have reversed his stand. Gradually the essay test declined from the position of dominance, but it still has a place in testing. Specifically, there are some subjects which simply

* Fred M. Smith and Sam Adams, *Educational Measurement for the Classroom Teacher* (New York: Harper & Row, Publishers, 1966), pp. 146–155.

could not be tested in any other way. Can you imagine taking a true-false test on creative writing? Many teachers find it useful to combine the essay test with other forms. There is no reason why this should not be done.

The *short-answer test,* sometimes referred to as "objective," is a fairly recent arrival on the testing scene. However, the short-answer test was not feasible until schools acquired duplication equipment. In using this type of test we frequently structure questions in such formats as true-false, multiple choice, completion, and matching. Many teachers devise their own types to fit their specific needs. This should be encouraged.

The short-answer test has several major strengths. It permits extensive sampling, is easy to score, and reduces the danger of student bluffing. However, there are some weaknesses. It encourages guessing—especially in true-false tests, in which odds are very good. Probably its greatest weakness as a teaching instrument is that it encourages fragmentary study. While it is possible to measure above the recall level with the short-answer test, many teachers test only on isolated bits of information. Hence the student is very likely to study according to this pattern. While facts are important, few teachers are willing to stop at that level. Specifically, if a teacher teaches at levels such as analysis or synthesis, he should be sure to test at these levels. This is very difficult if he limits his testing to the conventional short-answer types of questions.

Standardized Tests. The massive achievement test movement in the direction of standardized instruments grew out of a feeling that something was needed beyond teacher-made tests. The development of standardized tests dates back to the first decade of this century, when E. L. Thorndike and his associates produced a number of tests and scales of this type.

What is standardized about a standardized test? It is developed by an elaborate procedure so that each item has to prove its worth. Also, in a sense it is standardized in its method of production. Its content is the same for all who take it (no optional questions, for example). In addition, the method of administration is standardized, since the same set of directions and the same time limits apply to all tests groups. Finally, all scores are interpreted using the same yardstick, that is, the norms that apply for this test. So we see that a standardized test is standardized in practically all apsects of its production and usage.

To the classroom teacher the *test norms* of standardized tests are very important, since she uses them frequently. Usually the norms are set up in table form to facilitate the interpretation process. Actually, the norms represent nothing but the level of achievement of the "norm group." After the test has been published in its final form, a carefully selected group of students takes the test. This group may consist of several hundred to a thousand students who have been chosen as a sample to represent the "population." For example, the norms for fifth graders were drawn from a group of students who were selected, by a sampling process, to serve as the basis for future comparisons. Some people find an element of mystery about the norms, but the procedure for establishing them is comparatively simple.

Teachers sometimes are inclined to view the norms as goals and become quite excited when some of their students achieve ratings above grade level. There is no justification for such an interpretation, as the norms are in no way to be thought of as goals. They constitute a basis for interpreting scores and nothing else.

Certain standardized tests serve as "singles," while others are normally used as part of a collection of tests (a battery). However, each test is produced, used, and interpreted singly, even those that are part of a battery. Suppose, for example, that a high school biology teacher wants to use a standardized test in order to measure the achievement of his class. He would normally select a biology test only, since he would not have any real interest in a broad-spectrum measurement of his class. If, however, an elementary school wanted to survey the achievement of students in all the common areas of study, battery of tests would be used.

Many schools have a formally established pattern for administering batteries of achievement tests. A popular method is to give a complete battery to each student in the spring, near the end of the school year. Others test in the fall, shortly after school begins, while still others do both fall and spring testing. Which is better? The answer depends entirely upon the proposed objectives.

Intelligence tests

The story is told of the professor who was asked to define an intelligence test. He answered that an intelligence test is the instrument used to determine one's intelligence quotient (IQ). Later he was asked to define IQ and answered that it was the end result of taking an intelligence test. This is illustrative of the confusion that exists in the field of intelligence measurement.

If we impute to intelligence tests the power to measure innate ability (a very doubtful assumption, incidentally), one still might raise the question whether or not this is what the teacher needs to know. As a result of certain discussions of this sort, we now find that the trend is toward measuring "academic aptitude" rather than a somewhat more abstract thing called "intelligence."

What is an intelligence test? Essentially it is merely another assigned task—just as is true of any test. It is hoped that the intelligence test will give us some insight concerning level of performance on academic tasks that we could reasonably expect from a particular student. This is of great interest to the teacher.

The earliest work on intelligence testing was done by Alfred Binet, a French psychologist. After several false starts, including use of such tools as astrology and palmistry, he arrived at the conclusion that the best way to measure intelligence was to observe a youngster as he tried to cope with a problem-type situation. The scales Binet developed early in this century were revised and expanded by a group of workers at Stanford University, and the new version was issued as the Stanford-Binet test. Incidentally, this test always has been of the kind that must be given individually. Further, the giving of the test requires great skill and specialized training. Hence, the Stanford-Binet test is not designed for wholesale usage.

Early in World War I the military appealed to the nation's psychologists for help. Large numbers of people were entering the service, and processing their papers was an overwhelming task. The specific request was for an "intelligence test" that could be given to large groups. From this request grew Army Alpha and Army Beta, the first group tests of this sort. Army Beta was designed specifically for those who did not have proficiency in the English language, particularly for the foreign-born and illiterates.

Since the development of Army Alpha and Army Beta, a large number of intelligence tests have appeared on the market. They have undergone changes in order to account for changes in the theories of intelligence. Binet saw intelligence as a one-factor kind of entity. Spearman saw two factors. Later, Thurstone proposed six factors. The number keeps growing. Guilford has proposed a three-dimensional model yielding 120 different mental abilities. Now, if one proposes to measure intelligence, he must first decide which kind or kinds he shall measure. Intelligence is somewhat like the structure of the atom—the more we learn about it, the more complex it becomes.

Other tests and scales

In addition to the array of tests designed to measure achievement and intelligence, there are many others available. Some of these are called scales rather than tests, since the items do not have predetermined correct answers.

Personality Scales. It is almost as hard to arrive at a universally accepted definition of personality as it is to define intelligence. Yet considerable attention has been given to the development of instruments for personality study. One of these is the *inventory*. This is essentially a long list of statements or questions to which the student responds. While there are circumstances under which such inventories can yield useful information, their value to the classroom teacher is marginal. There is always the problem of different interpretations of statements by different individuals. Also, some students may give the answer they feel is expected, rather than the one that is true for them.

Another approach to personality testing is the *projective technique*. Here a picture, ink blot, or other stimulus is used to evoke a response in an unstructured situation. A trained psychologist can assess certain psychological characteristics by analyzing the responses. These instruments are clinical and are not recommended for use by the teacher unless he has had specialized training in their use.

Another technique that is sometimes useful is the *sociogram*, although it is more adapted to the study of groups than of individuals. The teacher might ask a question like, "With which person in the class would you most like to prepare a report?" Frequently, each student is asked to list his first, second, and third choices. By carefully studying the results, the teacher can extract interesting—and potentially useful—information about his group.

Interest Assessment. The study of student interests has been under way for many years. Yet we still do not have totally reliable instruments for this purpose. One problem, of course, is that interests frequently are "here today and gone tomorrow," so that conclusions are necessarily tentative.

Two instruments that have been widely used in the study of interests are the Strong Vocational Interest Blank and the Kuder Preference Record. Many teachers feel that it is good for students to use such instruments, since the mere usage may stimulate the student to think seriously about his own interests. Also, the actual "scores" or results can be of value to the student, although frequently these merely confirm what the student already knows about himself.

Skill Tests and Observations. In some areas of study, a major instructional goal is the development of certain skills. You can readily associate this with fields like home economics, physical education, industrial arts, laboratory phases of science, and others. In such cases, the teacher tests by observing students as they work. In a vocational course in radio repair, students were taught the methods used in "troubleshooting" a radio. The test was to have the student locate the trouble with a defective radio. He was rated not only on reaching the right conclusion, but also on the speed with which he handled the task, the amount of lost motion involved, and various other factors.

In testing of skills, the teacher must be observant and must have a systematic method of approach. It is important that the student knows in advance the basis upon which the test is developed. There should be no mystery in this type of testing.

TESTING IN TEACHING

As has been mentioned earlier, testing is, or should be, closely related to teaching. One undergraduate student in teacher education put it this way: "If you give a test, [and] then proceed to teach in exactly the same way you would have had you *not* given it, then you should not have given it at all." While this may be an oversimplification, it is an important principle.

Useful in motivation

What are the motives of the teacher in giving a test? One teacher gave her class a test as punishment because they had been "naughty." Some might be inclined to use the test as an instrument of coercion to get the class working. This latter approach, if handled in an affirmative way, could be thought of as motivation. Many students are inclined to become very casual in their work unless there are frequent tests. A few do not need it, but large numbers of students actually require this form of stimulation. Hence, it is good teaching to supply it.

Preparing for a test can be a good learning experience. There may be some class review, for example. Sometimes this degenerates into time-killing, but it can be a good teaching method when used sparingly and for short periods. Even more important is the individual review. The test gives the individual an incentive to try to fill in the gaps in his own learning. Incidentally, there is nothing wrong with devoting some class time to this.

How do you go about preparing students for a test? Certainly you should avoid threats and "scare talk." Furthermore, the students have a right to know generally what the test will be like. There should be no doubt as to the block of content to be covered. There should be ample advance notice for all major tests. Generally students, especially older ones need to know the type of test for which they are preparing. For example, if a student is preparing for an essay test, his study will be quite different from what it would be in preparing for a short-answer test. Do you see why?

As you can see, much of the teaching value of a test is based not upon the test *per se* but upon the activity that precedes it. The relearning that commonly occurs in preparing for a test is usually more permanent than is first-contact learning. Also, if we are to make maximum use of the pretest learning, it follows that we should test frequently.

Useful in diagnosis

A very important aspect of the work of the teacher is diagnosis. Since learning happens only to individuals, learning difficulties can have meaning only in reference to individuals. Just as a medical doctor is concerned with the location and treatment of physical difficulties, so the teacher is concerned with learning difficulties. Tests can be very helpful in this phase of teaching.

Tests Designed for Diagnosis. There are special diagnostic tests available to teachers. Some textbooks or teacher's manuals to accompany texts incorporate diagnostic tests at intervals. Certain texts in elementary mathematics, for example, have short diagnostic tests interspersed throughout the books. These are designed to help the student spot his own difficulty. Then he is referred to certain pages for additional work as needed. Also, there are diagnostic tests that are available through commerical sources. Then, of course, the teacher can always prepare such tests for his own class.

A diagnostic test differs from an achievement test in a variety of ways. Probably the most important are (1) the diagnostic test covers material intensively, and (2) as a result of this intensive treatment, the diagnostic test is usually limited in scope. Let us apply this to elementary mathematics again. If we wanted to test a student diagnostically in the process of addition, we would have to design our test to include every principle of addition, not just a sampling of them. It would follow that, to keep the test of reasonable length, we probably would not cover anything except addition in this test.

The Use of Diagnostic Tests. It should be kept in mind that the diagnostic test is not just another test. Hence there are certain phases of teaching in which this test is not of much help. For example, it should not be used in arriving at grades. Probably the unique feature of this test is that it spots patterns of errors. It is only as we become aware of such patterns that we can design remedial work for the student. Another characteristic of the diagnostic test is that it ignores such matters as "class average." Diagnosis is an individual process. Hence the diagnostic test is of interest only in the degree to which it points out weaknesses of individual students.

While the formal diagnostic test is of unique design, any test can serve certain purposes in diagnosis. If the teacher will go beyond "number right" or "number wrong" and look for patterns of errors on the part of individuals, he is making a diagnostic application to the test. It is assumed that, having located specific difficulties, the teacher would then design remedial work to help overcome them. At the risk of over-generalizing, the most important "diagnostic tool" is an observant teacher.

Useful in classification

Who decides what level of work is associated with which grade? Obviously, nobody does, since there are no established criteria. As long as we deal with a fairly stable school population, this usually does not become a pressing problem. However, let us consider a specific case. A large elementary school is located near a major military installation. Due to transfer of service personnel, the school population changes constantly. To add to the confusion, new students come in from all sorts of schools located in all parts of the world. The principal of the school in question has learned that he cannot place a student in a particular grade solely because that was his grade previously. The principal gives the new student a battery of achievement tests, then assigns him to the grade to which apparently he belongs.

Suppose that you, a new teacher, needed to make use of some form of ability grouping in your class. It would require weeks or months of careful observation on your part. However, if you have files of test results on your students, you have something to start on. Or suppose your school wants to establish remedial classes for students or classes for rapid learners. One of your better sources of information is the file of achievement test results for each student.

Useful in teacher self-evaluation

We have a common misconception that test results give information only about students. Frequently there is also a message for the teacher if he is willing to look for it.

A particular elementary school teacher works in a school which has for years given a battery of achievement tests near the end of the school term. Each year, this teacher's students compare very favorably with national norms in all subject areas except one—mathematics. As you would surmise, this teacher does not like mathematics, and she does not do a good job of teaching it. As applied to self-evaluation, these test results have a very clear, obvious meaning for this teacher, specifically, that she is doing a poor job in one subject area. In her case, the message has been ignored for many years.

Ideally, the teacher should examine test results for patterns of achievement or nonachievement that should have impact on the teaching process. Then he should make an honest effort to do something about deficiencies.

EVALUATING STUDENTS

Just as we associate teaching with testing, so must we associate teaching with evaluating. How do we relate testing and evaluating? A common illustration has to do with the man who set out to build a boat in his cellar. By means of a ruler or yardstick, he took the necessary measurements of the boat and of the cellar door (testing). Then he had to exercise judgment in deciding whether the boat would pass through the door (evaluating). The most obvious form of evaluation in the average school is in the matter of assigning marks at the end of a grading period.

Evaluation involves a variety of factors

Did you ever have a teacher who would "count off" for gum-chewing? Or for behavioral problems? Or for attitude? Some teachers are inclined to set up such elaborate grading procedures that even they do not understand them.

Tests. In a great many classrooms, tests are a major factor in grading. This is probably defensible, although it is possible to develop an overdependence on test results. What does this do to the youngster who gets very nervous on tests, hence does not give a true picture of his level of achievement?

Other Bases. Many teachers consider homework in assigning grades. Others depend upon projects, class reports, and related items. Grades should indicate student progress toward goals. Any evidence of such progress can help the teacher in the evaluation process. Some English teachers, for example, depend to a large extent upon themes as indicators of progress. The shop teacher has to depend largely upon completed projects for this purpose.

Teacher Judgment. Regardless of the amount of data the teacher might have recorded in a grade book, there finally comes the moment when he has to apply judgment and come up with a grade. No grading process can be so elaborate as to spare the teacher this task. Many school systems have developed guidelines to assist the teacher in this matter, and they can be most helpful. However, they can only help—they cannot to the job for the teacher.

The area of student evaluation is a big and important one. In many teacher education programs, students take a course in "tests and measures." It is to be hoped that, as a teacher, you will take the task of evaluation very seriously. When handled in a casual manner, it can create endless problems for the teacher and for the administration.

Bases of evaluation should be made known

A teacher is inviting problems when he surrounds his grading procedure with an aura of mystery. Even the good students become suspicious! A grading system should be relatively simple, and it should be made known to anyone who is interested. Essentially, the grade is a communications device. But if it is arrived at in a very roundabout way, just what does it communicate?

Many teachers develop some sort of point system for grading purposes. Early in the school year, the students are briefed on this system. Then each assignment that is to influence the grade is given a point value. This, too, is made known to the student. Then at any time during a grading period, it is possible for the interested student to see "how he stands on points."

Parents frequently inquire about grades, and they have a perfect right to do so. However, it is not possible for the teacher to devote long periods of time to explaining grading systems. Hence it is a good idea to have a system of evaluation that can be explained in a fairly brief conference. It is also important that this explanation not require a great many technical terms.

It is important that the school administrator be clear on a teacher's grading system. Frequently questions will be referred to him instead of the teacher. If he is in a position to provide an explanation, this will represent a considerable saving of time on the part of the teacher.

EVALUATING TEACHERS

Who grades teachers? Generally, nobody does. Yet there are situations in which it is important to have some sort of an evaluation of the work of a teacher. This is a very difficult task, a task which is far from complete at this point.

Success is hard to define

In measurement tests, a point of emphasis is that the grade or mark should indicate the progress of the student toward certain specific goals. But what *is* the goal of the teacher? It is easy to fall back on generalities—"to promote the growth of the student to his maximum potential," etc. However, goals that are usable in an evaluation situation need to be specific, not general. Hence one of the difficulties in teacher evaluation lies in the problems we encounter in defining the teacher's goals.

Another factor is that, even if we could agree on evaluative goals, there would still be no standard approach in working toward those goals. There are many routes but no foolproof directions. You have probably known teachers who achieved excellent results from highly unorthodox methods. The personality of the teacher is an important factor in his success, yet this, too, is hard to "pin down." Another aspect of this problem is that the success of the teacher is vitally affected by the nature of his students. While a teacher might be doing a remarkable job with a class of slow learners, his success is not likely to be detectable by any of the standard measuring devices.

It is easy for an administrator to evaluate a teacher on the basis of such factors as cooperation with administrators, cooperation with other teachers, and effectiveness of parent relations. All of these are important, and these are factors upon which the administrator would have some information. You will note, however, that none of these is directly concerned with the work of the teacher with students; yet this should be the prime consideration.

Someone has to evaluate teachers

Situations sometimes occur in which decisions have to be made that are based (presumably) upon the effectiveness of a teacher. First, there is the matter of initial employment. In most parts of the country, the prospective teacher will have had a course in student teaching. His work here has to be evaluated, and this evaluation frequently is an important factor in the matter of placement. Also, in many schools, teachers serve for a probationary period before they gain tenure. Someone has to decide during this period if appointment should be allowed to become permanent.

Some school systems have tried teacher evaluation as a basis for merit salary increases. In many lines of work such a system is entirely feasible. However, in teaching it has met with very limited success. It is doubtful if such a system, despite its obvious theoretical merit, will enjoy wide success until we find better ways to evaluate teachers.

Do any civic clubs in your area confer "Teacher of the Year" or similar awards? If so, someone has to decide who is worthy of such recognition. It is hoped that professional advancement represents a form of recognition of success. So, despite the difficulties of the process, teacher evaluation goes on constantly.

Some procedures

Some school systems have developed elaborate checklists to be used in teacher evaluation. These normally include "criteria for success," with degrees of achievement to be checked. Frequently more than one person will evaluate a teacher—possibly the principal and a district supervisor. The prime weakness of system is obvious—the people who are doing the evaluating are not the people the teacher has been teaching. So why not have the students evaluate the teacher? This has been tried, especially in higher education. Problems arise almost immediately. Is the student likely to be objective? Is he really in a position to evaluate the teacher? So, you see, we not only have the question of "how?" in teacher evaluation. There is also the matter of "by whom?"

Many school systems use a less formal procedure which is adequate for their purposes. Just as there is a cumulative file for the students, there is such a file for each teacher. Pertinent correspondence, anecdotal records, newspaper clippings, and any other material that will reflect something of the teacher's work over a period of years is filed. As questions of an evaluative nature arise, the person who is to evaluate will at least have something to use in the process.

QUESTIONS AND ACTIVITIES

1. Do you agree with the statement that "testing is teaching?" Defend your position.
2. Do the schools of your community have programs of standardized testing? If so, what do they consist of? What use is made of the results?
3. What is your concept of intelligence? Do you know of any tests that will measure it?
4. What are some unique problems of grading at the elementary school level? High school level? College level?
5. It has been proposed that students evaluate their teachers. Do you see this as a good idea? Why?
6. On the basis of your own library research, describe changes that have occurred in intelligence testing over the past several decades.

SOME SUGGESTED READINGS

Bond, Guy L., and Eva Bond Wagner, *Teaching the Child to Read*, New York: The Macmillan Company, 1950.

Ford, Paul L., *The New England Primer*, Dodd, 1897.

Kottmeyer, William, *Teacher's Guide for Remedial Reading*, St. Louis: Webster Publishing Co., 1959.

Michaelis, John U., *Social Studies for Children in a Democracy* (4th ed.), Englewood Cliffs, N.J.: Prentice-Hall, Inc., 1968.

Minnich, Harvey C., *William Holmes McGuffey and His Readers*, New York: American Book Company, 1936.

Russell, David H., *Children Learn to Read*, Boston: Ginn and Company, 1949.

Russell, David H., and Etta E. Karp, *Reading Aids Through the Grades: Three Hundred Developmental Reading Activities*, New York: Teachers College, Columbia University, Bureau of Publications, 1961.

Shipp, Donald E., and Sam Adams, *Developing Arithmetic Concepts and Skills*, Englewood Cliffs, N.J.: Prentice-Hall, Inc., 1964.

12

LEARNING AND TEACHING

While this section of the text is devoted to the general topic of teaching, it would be unrealistic to disregard the "state of the art" of learning. Frequently we have referred to the teaching-learning process. In many applications this is defensible despite the fact that much of what we learn is self-taught. Can you imagine a truly successful teacher who does not know anything about learning?

SOME EARLY VIEWS OF LEARNING

Earlier in this book we made incidental reference to some early concepts of the learning process. We would not be justified in classing these rudimentary ideas even as theories, since they were primarily intuitive. It is only in comparatively modern times that psychologists have engaged in systematic research on how we learn.

Learning as memorization

As was pointed out in our discussion of the *New England Primer*, the goal in many of our early schools was total memorization. Surely by the time a student spent several terms on the same relatively small book, he must have been able to recite it backward and forward.

However, it was not just in reading class that learning was equated with memorization. Arithmetic was taught in essentially the same way. An early textbook in this field* included an addition table on page 2 and a multiplication table on the next page. Further, it was suggested that no student proceed beyond this point until he had achieved mastery of these tables. Do you know of any students who never would have gone past page 3?

In addition to the memorization of tables, there was much emphasis on memorizing rules. These were usually in heavy print so that they stood out. Thus, viewing learning as memorizing, a good memorizer could have advanced quite rapidly through this type of material without understanding anything.

* Nathan Daboll, *Schoolmaster's Assistant* (E. and E. Hasford, 1821).

The study of grammar was deemed to be quite important. However, it was confined largely to learning definitions and rules. The related field of spelling also stressed memorization for later "spelling out loud." A teacher took great pride in a student who could spell Constantinople, prestidigitation, or phthisic, even though he might not be able to spell words of daily usage.

We still require students to learn basics, although we earnestly try to avoid calling it memorization. The key difference is that we no longer regard the memorization of abstract or unrelated material as an end in itself.

Learning as mental discipline

Another concept of learning that dominated America's schools for many years was that of mental discipline. Proponents of this view held that the mind was comparable to a muscle, and the only way to develop a muscle was through strenuous exercise. Hence, it was assumed that the development of the mind could be achieved by having the student wrestle with extremely difficult subject matter.

A major study area during the period in question was mental arithmetic. In a textbook* that was very popular during the latter part of the 19th century, the prescribed method of teaching for mental discipline was outlined. It consisted of the following steps: (1) the teacher reads the problem; (2) the student, writing nothing, thinks through the problem, then raises his hand to indicate that he has reached a solution; (3) the teacher calls upon a student who rises, repeats the problem, and gives the solution. The type of problem solved is illustrated by the following: A man lost 2/5 of his hens and found that if he sold 2/3 of the remainder at cost, he would receive 40 dimes, but if he kept 15 and sold 2/3 of the remainder, he would receive 20 dimes; how many did he have?

You will note that a problem had to meet only one criterion, that is, it had to be difficult. The element of practicality was of no concern. Consider, for example, how long a person might continue in the chicken business without encountering the

---

* Edward Brooks, *The New Moral Mental Arithmetic* (Philadelphia: Christopher Sower Company, 1873).

type of problem shown above. The fact that students were denied writing materials while working on such problems merely meant that added mental exercise could be thus obtained.

Another aspect of the mental discipline theory was the _assumption of transfer._ It was thought that mental gymnastics in one subject area produced results that would carry over into all areas. Hence, a student who developed proficiency in mental arithmetic was thereby becoming a better student in all subject areas. Can you think of any subject areas in the modern elementary or secondary school in which traces of mental discipline are still discernible?

Learning as punishment

There has not been a period in educational history when learning as punishment constituted a major movement; yet the two have been related in many classrooms.

Consider, for example, the teacher who doubles the assignment to "reward" misbehavior. Some teachers have even gone so far as to design special assignments for individual students, the length of each being determined by "how bad he has been." Other manifestations of this attitude are orders such as: "stay after school for an hour of study time," "stay in during recess," and others you could probably add. Still another way in which learning has been associated with punishment is in the area of motivation: "If you don't know the multiplication tables by tomorrow, you're going to get a licking."

In cases in which a student had to put in extra study time as punishment, the subject areas used most often by teachers were spelling and arithmetic. Do you think that there was any relationship between this fact and the fact that these two subjects were pretty generally disliked by students?

SOME CURRENT VIEWS ABOUT
LEARNING

Systematic studies of learning never cease. Consequently the body of knowledge about the learning process undergoes continuous change. However, there are some generally accepted principles of learning which are outlined in this section.

Readiness

The term "readiness" is largely self-descriptive. In the educational sense it generally means that a student has acquired the mental and physical skills and understandings that are basic to an assigned task, that he is motivated, and that he is psychologically prepared to move to the new assignment.

Psychological Aspects. You have probably heard the expression "reading readiness." This is only one kind of readiness, but it can be used as an illustration. In earlier years the first-grade teacher was very likely to pressure students in her new class to learn to read at the earliest possible moment. It was noted that some learned much more slowly than others. Also it was observed by many teachers that the youngster who was reluctant to learn this skill was usually just as reluctant to use it—in short, he did not like to read. It was postulated that such a student might become a better reader if he were relieved of the pressure to get started at it early in the school year—that is, if he learned to read after he was ready.

This realization has greatly influenced the teaching of reading. The modern first-grade teacher is likely to surround a student with interesting and attractive reading matter. The youngster observes his fellow students as they read and notes their obvious enjoyment of it. He engages in games in which the ability to read would be useful. As an outgrowth of these and other environmental factors, he develops "reading readiness." It is important to note, however, that the teacher has not simply put him in storage to await the magic moment of readiness. He has carefully arranged an environment which promotes its development.

This psychological conditioning for learning is of importance in all subject areas and at all grade levels. However, our ways of promoting it vary, depending upon many factors. Do you recall the case, previously mentioned, in which a lower elementary school teacher introduced the process of borrowing in subtraction by confronting students with exercises requiring borrowing? She made constructive use of the resulting confusion. How did her method relate to the promotion of readiness?

Skills Aspect. In an adult education class, a certain student announced that his goal was to learn long division. He did not want to waste any time on such details as multiplication or subtraction; he wanted to go directly to long division. You will note that, in certain respects, readiness was established because this individual was highly motivated. However, he definitely lacked readiness in the area of requisite skills. Hence there was no way in which he could succeed in his task.

In many subject areas the student builds each year's successes directly upon the learnings of previous years. But what happens if he did not acquire such learnings the previous year? Obviously, the gaps must be filled in prior to any major forward progress.

At the risk of oversimplification, we can consider readiness as based upon two questions: (1) Is he in the proper frame of mind for learning? (2) Does he know enough to go into this new learning experience? Suppose that a student fails to meet one of these conditions. What is the responsibility of the teacher?

Knowledge about the individual learner important

Does it strike you as odd that, during the same general period of educational development, we learned to group students into grades while placing increased emphasis on individual differences? We know that a teacher working with 30 students in a class cannot totally individualize instruction. Yet there are many ways in which he can allow for the fact that he is teaching 30 *people* rather than teaching one *group*. The effective teacher constantly seeks ways in which he can learn about the individual students with whom he works and, having learned, can use his knowledge in the teaching process.

The Student's Rate of Learning. After you have taught a class for a fairly short period, you will have located the students who are at the extremes of the learning spectrum—the slow learner and the rapid learner. However, each student of the so-called average group also has his own learning pattern. It is important that the teacher know about this. Many experienced teachers can predict, prior to class, which of their students will have difficulty with certain content. With this kind of background, the teacher can frequently adapt his instruction to the individuals in such a way as to preclude many of the learning problems that might arise.

How does the teacher acquire this kind of knowledge about a student? There is the cumulative file of test results and related information; there is the scholastic record; there are colleagues who have taught him earlier. But most important, the teacher must be observant, and he must see the student as an individual —not as one of the 30 names listed alphabetically in the class roll.

The Student's Attention Span. How can a teacher tell when his students are no longer giving attention to a class activity? Some fidget; others start conversations; others engage in "excessive notetaking," which usually means they are writing letters or doing some work for another class; others merely daydream. But an alert teacher is acutely conscious of all symptoms that indicate the class is no longer "with him." One reaction is for the teacher to demand attention. However, it is generally more effective if the teacher will give the class a change of activity for a while. After all, attention span has physical reality and cannot be ignored.

To what extent is attention span a class characteristic? Some teachers will generalize about it, with expressions like, "That is a very inattentive class." One ninth grade science teacher recently remarked that the girls had an attention span of about twenty minutes, and the boys had an attention span of about twenty seconds. However, despite efforts toward generalization, attention span is an individual matter. Hence, it is important for the teacher to be conscious of this factor as it applies to each student in his class.

The Student's Response Patterns. If we are to be of service to a student faced with a learning task, we have to know something about the way he reacts to a variety of situations. For example, a student who is carrying out an operation incorrectly certainly needs to be corrected. However, some students bitterly resent outright correction. Some might accept it without reaction, while others expect and even appreciate it.

In the matter of student conduct, we run into a broad range of reactions. A simple correction for improper conduct can arouse responses varying from an honest apology to outright rebellion. A teacher can avoid all sorts of problems along this line if he knows his students well enough to use the approach that works for each student.

Elementary school teachers frequently encounter this same difference in response. A particular game strikes one student as being great fun while another considers the same activity somewhat silly.

The Student's Interests and Motivation. One of the surest ways of establishing a good learning situation with a student is to utilize his interests. A student who would have little interest in a law of physics when taught in the abstract would see the whole thing in a totally different way when related to an interest or hobby of his. Very frequently this same approach can be highly motivational. A boy who is interested in aeronautics would like to prepare a class report on jet fuels; a girl interested in becoming a dietician could assume a leadership role in an experiment comparing the effects of different diets on laboratory animals. Obviously, such a procedure can be of value to a teacher only if he knows the individual students in his class well enough to enlist them at the proper times.

Learning considered to be behavioral

Learning is intimately related to behaving. As changes occur in what we know, corresponding changes occur in the way we act. In an extensive study by Benjamin Bloom and his associates, behavior was classified into three types: the cognitive domain, concerning itself primarily with mental functions; the affective domain, including such things as attitudes and beliefs; and the psychomotor domain, centering around physical activity.

To illustrate the behavioral aspects of one type of learning, let us examine the levels of behavior in the cognitive domain. (1) Knowledge. The behavior is essentially that of being able to recall information. (2) Comprehension. The behavior is generally described as "understanding." (3) Application. The behavior implied here is that of using in a concrete situation that which has been learned at the knowledge or comprehension level. (4) Analysis. The behavior is the breaking down of concepts into their component parts. (5) Synthesis. This behavior is essentially that of creative thinking. (6) Evaluation. The behavior is the making of value judgments.*

Success vital to learning

In any assigned task, some degree of success is important. Learning is no exception. Imagine yourself in the situation in which, day after day, you tried to cope with a task that was completely beyond your capacity. You can easily imagine that your enthusiasm for the task would fall to the vanishing point as soon as you realized the situation. If you continued on this task, you would likely develop a feeling of resentment toward those responsible for your assignment to the task in question. How would this relate to the problem of the dropout?

Yet many students go to school year after year encountering nothing but failure. Consider the case of a fifth-grade boy. For two years he had not made a single passing grade in mathematics. As a result, he felt completely defeated by a situation from which he did not know how to escape. He was not the type to create a behavioral problem; he daydreamed. In short, having accepted defeat as his permanent lot in this subject, he simply "tuned out" and thought of more pleasant things.

How would the teacher deal with a case such as the one just described? If the youngster is starved for a taste of success, it may be necessary for the teacher to contrive a situation in which such success can be experienced. In this case, a tutor worked with the lad for a while and reverted him—without saying so—to a second grade textbook. With such easy material, it was possible for the boy to move forward without difficulty. He was working at his grade level after a fairly short time span, simply because he had started far enough back to become a "successful" student.

Not only is success important; recognition for that success is vital. People of all ages crave some form of recognition, and this is especially true for both elementary and secondary

---

* For further information regarding this aspect of learning, the student is referred to Benjamin Bloom's *Taxonomy of Educational Objectives, Handbook I: Cognitive Domain* and *Handbook II: Affective Domain*. Both were published by David McKay Co., Inc. (New York), the first in 1956 and the second in 1964.

school students. However, insincere compliments for a mediocre job do not work. Even small children see through this. Rather, the teacher should seek ways to help a student actually achieve at a high level on some phase of work, then reward him with recognition. It is especially helpful if fellow students take part in the recognition of a job well done.

Incidentally, the importance of success in learning is brought out in programmed materials. In the programmed book the student is led forward in minute steps, so designed as to give him every chance of success. The reinforcement that occurs with the feeling of achievement as the student works through a sequence of programmed material is a vital phase of learning.

Learning an active process

We have seen that learning is related to behavior. Yet behavior is an active, not a passive, process. In short, learning occurs as a result of something we do; it is an outcome of an "activity." Obviously this type of activity is not necessarily related to physical motion.

While the role of spectator is quite adequate for amusement, it usually falls short as an approach to learning. Let us illustrate with the case of a classroom film. Miss A simply says, "And now we will have a movie." Each student feels that he is meeting his responsibility simply by contributing his physical presence. Miss B also uses a film, but she assigns specific questions for which they are to seek answers while watching, or she announces that there will be a short test based upon the film. In either case, she is changing the role of the student from spectator to participant. There is little doubt as to which teacher will better aid learning through use of the film.

Did you ever have a teacher who was so intent upon your learning the material that she practically did it for you? Teacher domination can actually retard learning. Such a teacher accepts the premise that "learning is an active process," then proceeds to provide the activity herself. In a good learning situation, a student has an opportunity to grope around a bit. He even exercises his prerogative to get utterly confused occasionally. A teacher who rushes prematurely to his rescue, thereby denying him the privilege of working his way out of the situation, is denying the student a valuable learning experience. We encounter frequent references to the "discovery method," especially in subject areas such as mathematics. This involves a minimum of telling or explaining on the part of the teacher. Some teachers, however, are so conditioned to the use of the "let me show you" method that they really cannot use discovery.

It is a task of major proportions to get some students actively involved in the learning process. Some concede defeat without trying. Others are happy in the role of observer. Some simply do not want to be bothered. One of the real challenges to the teacher is that of seeking out ways to "get to" those students who do not have any particular desire to learn the material at hand.

Challenges stimulate learning

Some students who fail to respond to any of the usual types of assignments respond well to a problem situation. We are not referring to the usual textbook problem but rather to a real question without an obvious answer—a question that has meaning in the life of the student. One junior high school science teacher likes to run a demonstration before her class without speaking a word. Then the students work on the challenging question, "What has been shown?" A physics teacher brought in some glass cubes, wondered aloud what their index of refraction was, further commented that he doubted that any of the students could devise a system of measuring it, then left the class to its own devices for a time. The class response to the challenge left little to be desired.

Teachers in practically all situations can stimulate learning by challenge. It is more a point of view than a procedure. If a teacher approaches a problem situation with the "this is how you do it" type of thinking, there is little challenge to the student. But if her approach is "how would you do it?", there can be real stimulation to learning.

Challenges to create can be as real as challenges to solve. The writing of a class paper, the preparation of a report or an art exhibit—these and many others offer endless opportunities to challenge creativity. Schools are sometimes criticized for discouraging those who are creative, and in some classrooms this may be true. However, it does not *have* to be true. Many students are eager to display their creative ability and will do so if properly challenged.

Parallel to the challenge to learn and the challenge to create is the challenge to lead. In many school situations we find the same people preempting leadership positions over and over again. Frequently there is excellent leadership potential available but, for some reason, the persons are not motivated to assume a leading role. If this is to be avoided, then it is necessary that a conscious effort be made by teachers to help all students see the challenge of leadership, then motivate them to try. This does *not* mean that the teacher meddles in student government elections. Rather, he provides leadership opportunities in class or club activities with which he is directly involved, and he tries to interest many students in them.

Learning happens to individuals

This principle has been mentioned before. However, it is important enough to merit reemphasis. In America's schools, we are constantly preoccupied with the task of coping with sheer numbers of students. Schools are classified for various purposes on the basis of enrollment. Yet, in our concern about numbers, we have to keep in mind the basic fact that learning is *not* a a group process. It is the ultimate of individualization. Thus the modern teacher lives in the midst of a dichotomy of concerns—for the group and for the people who constitute the group. Sometimes these concerns support each other, but frequently they are in direct conflict.

TEACHING-LEARNING PROCESS

In the section dealing with current views of learning, an effort was made to involve teaching applications. However, certain aspects of the teacher's involvement with basic learning need special attention.

Good teaching seldom happens accidentally

This statement could not be justified if we said "never" instead of "seldom." There are occasions when the sudden inspiration or the totally unexpected teaching opportunity can promote good teaching and in a totally unanticipated manner. However, regardless of the education, skill, or experience of the teacher, he cannot proceed on the assumption that these opportunities will arise as he needs them.

Careful planning is a vital phase of good teaching. The nature of the planning is affected by age levels and other factors. The amount of detail in planning is influenced by the experience of the teacher. However, regardless of these and other variables, we can safely assume that a teacher who arrives in the classroom totally unprepared for his task is most unlikely to engage in good teaching.

In apparent contradiction to the above is the fact that a teacher must be willing and able to use effectively those "teachable moments" that do arise. A student teacher in a general science class spent hours planning his class discussion on thunderstorms. He brought elaborate written lesson plans to class. During the class period, a thunderstorm arose. Every topic in his plan was beautifully illustrated as the storm ran its course outside the classroom. The teacher was so concerned about living up to the letter of his written plan he was totally unaware of the "laboratory demonstration" that had been perfectly timed for his use. On the other hand, an elementary school teacher was leading a class discussion relating to animals when a large cat leaped up onto the window sill and stretched out in the sun for a nap. She immediately switched over to the cat as a topic and made very good use of the unexpected assistance.

The point that is worthy of emphasis here is that since the latter teacher had a lesson prepared, she would have had a good class even if the cat had not arrived. Yet she was flexible enough in her thinking to recognize and use the "teachable moment" that arose as a result of the cat's visit.

Teacher-learner relationships are important

In our attention to teaching and learning, we must not overlook the important relationships between the teacher and the learner. Such relationships, if they are to be constructive, must be sought. Again, one cannot depend upon luck or a timely accident for this purpose.

An attitude of helpful informality between teacher and student is important. Again, this does not happen with a class; rather, it happens with the individuals who constitute the class. Such a relationship can only grow out of a feeling of mutual respect between the persons involved. Did you ever know a teacher who demanded pupil respect but somehow failed to reciprocate?

Another phase of this relationship is the freedom of discussion which should prevail. Sometimes total frankness can be disruptive to a class discussion, but in private conversation there should be an open channel of discussion between teacher and student. A teacher who becomes ill at ease when a "forbidden topic" arises is not likely to establish this relationship.

A teacher who is to work constructively with a particular age group needs to be well acquainted with the traits of that age group. A teacher whose feelings are hurt over the flippant remark of a teen-ager or who sees a personal affront in the moodiness of an adolescent is very unlikely to be happy or successful in his relationships with such age groups.

QUESTIONS AND ACTIVITIES

1. Have you ever encountered any learning experiences which, in your opinion, were based upon mental discipline? Explain.

2. How would you propose to apply the concept of readiness in your own teaching?

3. Have you ever had a teacher who made effective use of the challenge as a teaching device? How?

4. What measures would you take in teaching a very inattentive class? Do you consider this to be a disciplinary problem?

5. Have you ever had a teacher whose assignments were too difficult for the class? Too easy? What problems resulted in each case?

6. In earlier courses, had you been required to memorize selections from literature? How many can you now

recite? How would you evaluate your own learning experience in this type of material?

7. Did you ever have the experience of "writing lines" as punishment? Did you learn anything? Explain.

SOME SUGGESTED READINGS

Alexander, William M., *Are You A Good Teacher?*, New York: Rinehart and Company, Inc., 1959.

Beck, Robert H., Walter W. Cook, and Nolan C. Kearney, *Curriculum in the Modern Elementary School*, Englewood Cliffs, N.J.: Prentice-Hall, Inc., 1960.

Lyman, Howard, *Test Scores and What They Mean*, Englewood Cliffs, N.J.: Prentice-Hall, Inc., 1963.

Michaelis, John U., *Social Studies for Children in a Democracy*, (4th ed.), Englewood Cliffs, N.J.: Prentice-Hall, Inc., 1968.

Russell, David H., *Children Learn to Read*, Boston: Ginn and Company, 1949.

Seashore, Harold G., "On Telling Parents About Test Results," *Test Service Bulletin*, No. 54, Psychological Corporation, 1956.

Shaw, Jack, and Olaf P. Anfinson, *Using Measurement in Education*, Ann Arbor, Mich.: J. W. Edwards, Publisher, Inc., 1961.

Smith, Fred M., and Sam Adams, *Educational Measurement for the Classroom Teacher*, New York: Harper & Row, Publishers, 1966.

13

DISCIPLINE
AND
TEACHING

We hear and read a great deal about problems of discipline in schools. These problems are very real. It would be a mistake to assume that they are new, although behavioral difficulties in schools have changed as a result of general sociological changes that have occurred. Further, the teacher's methods of dealing with such problems have been altered considerably in the past 50 years. We still debate the question concerning which method worked best.

Discipline is an integral part of teaching. Regardless of the level of scholarship achieved by the teacher, he will not be very effective until he has achieved good class order. A maxim often quoted by teachers of a few generations ago was, "If you can't control 'em, you can't larn 'em." While the grammar could be improved upon, the sense is as applicable now as it has ever been.

MEANING OF DISCIPLINE

If you should look up the term "discipline" in a dictionary, you would find that it has many meanings and shades of meaning. However, as we use it here, essentially it implies control. Even this term is variously interpreted. For example, the animal trainer in a circus, through the use of a system of rewards and punishments, achieves a type of control. The word discipline is derived from the Latin term *discere*, which means "to learn." This is the sense in which most teachers like to view it. Indeed, the achievement of good classroom order is a learning situation for student and teacher. The teacher who is to promote the right kind of learning views discipline in the context of "something to be taught."

Early concepts of discipline

In the Puritan community, the child was constantly reminded of his sinful nature. In the home, the church, and the school, he was subjected to stern and inflexible sets of rules. A basic principle was that the child should live under the rule of an absolute authority. Much has been written about this period in American education, but the outstanding aspect relative to discipline is the free use of corporal punishment. The birch rod was as important to the teacher as was any other "teaching material."

You will recall that the Massachusetts colony was Calvinist, while Virginia was settled by adherents of the Church of England. In the latter colony, a somewhat more tolerant view of the nature of man—hence, of children—prevailed. The discipline was fairly rigid but was administered in a more kindly, less brutal fashion.

In all of the early schools, discipline was external in nature —that is, it was something imposed upon the child by an outside agency. Little thought was given to the fact that this promoted resentment and rebellion. If such symptoms appeared, it simply meant that the punishment had not been adequate—a situation which was immediately corrected.

More recent concepts of discipline

Discipline problems are still with us and will be as long as we work with people. Further, no teacher, regardless of experience, is spared such problems. Beginning teachers frequently are vitally concerned with such matters. Consequently, should you become a teacher, you will be involved with problems of student behavior from the beginning to the end of your career.

One concept of discipline which is generally accepted is that "the best discipline comes from within." The weaknesses of a discipline imposed by an external agency are obvious. Many teachers and administrators stress the fact that they seek to develop intelligent self-control. As one teacher put it, the measure of the effectiveness of her system of classroom discipline was the conduct of her students when she was out of the room. There are situations, of course, when an imposed discipline is essential. However, this does not reduce the value of self-discipline as a goal.

Another widely accepted theory of discipline is that behavior is caused by something. Hence, a teacher seldom, if ever, deals with a behavioral problem which results solely because the student is out to give trouble. Frequently, careful observation on the part of the teacher will reveal the basic difficulty. Sometimes corrective action can be taken by the teacher; frequently it cannot. At any rate, an understanding of the root problem is very helpful in working with the student concerned.

If we accept the principle that discipline is something we teach, we must also accept the fact that there are several methods of teaching it. Just as there is no universal recipe for teaching English, so there is no magic formula for discipline. The development of skill in this phase of teaching requires a certain amount of groping on the part of the teacher. The system used by one of your former teachers or by your student-teaching supervisor would probably be unsatisfactory if you used it. You have to develop the method that works best for you.

Nobody can discipline a class for the teacher. Regardless of the strength of the principal, and regardless of his eagerness to help, he cannot maintain order in each classroom. He is a good resource in dealing with special problems, but the conditions that prevail in a particular classroom on a day-to-day (indeed, moment-to-moment) basis will necessarily be those established by the teacher.

What has happened to punishment in discipline? It is still with us in a variety of forms. Some schools still make use of the paddle or the strap. However, in many districts, corporal punishment in any form has been outlawed. When you become a teacher, you should become clear, before the school year begins, on the forms of disciplinary action available for your use. It can be most embarrassing if the sequence is reversed—that is, you use a form of discipline and then learn that it is illegal.

THE TEACHER AND DISCIPLINE

You might wonder why the teaching of discipline differs from the teaching of spelling. We teach toward goals. Some goals are fairly easy to achieve ("Learn to spell the following words"), while others are much more difficult ("Learn to behave!"). Consequently, while the teaching of discipline has certain points of similarity with other types of teaching, it also has many features that are unique.

The teaching of attitudes

We cannot generalize that behavioral problems on the part of students reflect negative attitudes, since many such problems arise as a result of carelessness or lack of thought. However, a continuous and prolonged disciplinary lapse must be based on something—frequently a faulty attitude. The teaching of attitudes is difficult; yet it is the responsibility of the teacher to try.

Deferred Satisfaction. It is the hope of the teacher that classroom discipline will be the outgrowth of individual self-discipline. One of the basic ingredients of intelligent self-control is an attitude of deferred satisfaction. Why go to college when I can get a job now? Why recopy the theme when the first draft is legible? Why do we keep drilling on signals for the football team when I already know them fairly well?

A member of the first-grade class had a birthday, and his mother brought cookies to school for the class. The question arose as to whether they should eat them at ten o'clock or wait until lunch. The skilled teacher handled the situation in such a way that they decided to wait. This was a type of instruction in discipline.

In helping a student develop self-discipline, it is essential that the teacher let the student decide. Self-discipline cannot be imposed by the teacher. Instead, he should establish situations in which the student must evaluate two outcomes (immediate *vs.* deferred) and hopefully decide wisely. Furthermore, this cycle must be repeated in a variety of situations. Think how much easier it would be for the teacher simply to tell the student what to do. Yet this would do little to promote student growth.

Consequences of Actions. There is always a tendency for youngsters to act on impulse. Parents and teachers constantly hear the expression, "I didn't think." While this may not be an acceptable explanation, it frequently is a very honest one. The ability to look ahead and envision likely outcomes is acquired, not innate. Some students insist upon learning this lesson the hard way. However, the teacher frequently can be of assistance.

A particular high school student took his school work very casually. Then when the time came to apply for admission to the college of his choice, he was promptly rejected on the basis of his record. An elementary school student had his arm in a cast because of a fracture. Complications arose because he had been playing football while wearing the cast. His explanation: "I didn't think."

Again, the role of the teacher is complex because merely telling does not help. However, the teacher can always raise such questions as, "Have you really thought this through?" and "Are you sure this is what you want to do?" If the proposed action is obviously wrong, a more direct form of intervention might be necessary. However, at the next opportunity, the teacher would be back with the same questions, hoping to promote self-discipline in the form of looking ahead.

Altruism. If a person lived in a world by himself, discipline would not be very important. While his acts would affect him, they would not affect anyone else. Hence, society would not need to intervene in the matter of setting standards of conduct.

Altruism, or concern for others, is a vital part of self-discipline. A junior high school teacher had to interrupt a class discussion to correct a student on a behavioral problem. Two minutes of class time were lost. Since the class had 30 students, sixty minutes of student instructional time were forfeited. Obviously, the student who created the problem was not very concerned about the welfare of his fellows.

Small children frequently are quite self-centered, with little regard for the welfare of others. The teacher must seek ways to broaden the youngster's pattern of concern. Incidentally, some people never learn this lesson and continue to live self-centered lives as adults.

Sense of Fair Play. Some young children object violently to taking turns. Some older students will resort to questionable tactics in order to win an election or an athletic contest. You sometimes hear such quotations as "Good guys finish last." Teachers should keep in mind that fair play frequently differs from "doing what comes naturally." Opportunities to promote fair play should be sought, then used to fullest advantage.

Property Rights. A willingness to accept the fact that other people have the right to own and control property needs to be taught. In some cases, stealing can be a problem. However, even more common are such practices as unauthorized borrowing or failure to return borrowed property.

Acceptance of Criticism. Nobody really likes to be criticized, yet all of us can profit by criticism. Some students have a glib explanation for any shortcomings. Others resent criticism, and some become definitely hostile over it. The teacher has to be critical on occasion. He should try to keep his criticism on a constructive level, then make every effort to teach a wholesome acceptance of it.

Fidelity to Promises. "I forgot it, but I'll be sure to bring it tomorrow." Any teacher has heard this expression. Sometimes this promise is kept, but frequently it is not. Equally important are promises made to parents or to other students. The teacher should try in any way possible to help the student understand the importance of promises and the need to fulfill them.

Obedience to Authority. In recent years we have seen a deterioration of this highly important phase of discipline. The teacher tries to give the student enough latitude to help him develop his own judgment. However, when the time comes for the exercise of authority, it is highly important that the student respond properly. Can you imagine what would happen in a large school if students defied authority at the time the building was on fire? Students are sometimes inclined to ask endless questions about the justification for a particular rule. If the circumstances permit an explanation, there is nothing wrong with giving one. However, in any social situation, there come times when we have to obey proper authority. This attitude has to be taught.

Acceptance of Defeat. It was recently said of a high school girl that, "She's very nice as long as she wins." This particular youngster was an only child of highly indulgent parents. Consequently, she usually "won." Yet many of our most valuable lessons emerge from defeats. In a commercial laundry, there was a "lost clothes" room. Above the door was this sign: "Have faith, ye mortals who enter here; all is not lost." This point of view generally is important to the loser—all is not lost. Some students, in defeat, are best left to suffer in silence; others need consolation. The role of the teacher is determined by his knowledge of his students.

Punctuality. Did you ever notice that some people are always late? Being on time—or being late—is a matter of habit. An important aspect of self-discipline is punctuality. The teacher's role in promotion of good habits in this regard is somewhat complex. However, once a reasonable standard is established, it should be adhered to as closely as possible.

The importance of good relationships

There are situations in which every move made by the teacher in the area of control arouses resentment. Further, this resentment can affect all or practically all of the students in a class. Other teachers can handle the same types of situations and the class actually enjoys them. What is the difference?

The prime difference lies in the kind of relationship that exists between teacher and students. If there is a feeling of mutual respect, if the teacher is known to be fair—in short, if there is a wholesome and constructive approach used in handling a behavioral problem—things usually work out well. If, however, the teacher permits himself to be petty or sarcastic, or if he is endlessly making corrections, problems are to be expected.

How is the teacher to establish good relationships? Primarily the problem is one of teacher attitude. The term used earlier is important—respect. If the teacher honestly respects the members of his class as individuals, the members are likely to reciprocate. Also, every action taken must be constructive, designed to promote the growth of the student. Note that this eliminates any attitude of vengeance or "getting even" on the part of the teacher. Incidentally, the teacher's relationships with students outside of class can be most helpful in establishing good in-class rapport.

Proper relations with parents can be an important factor in good discipline. Very likely the negative attitudes displayed by students at school are being displayed—in more pronounced form—at home. The teacher and the parent can be mutually helpful in their efforts to arrive at causes and corrective actions in this regard.

Causes of poor pupil adjustment

It has been mentioned earlier that behavior problems are caused by something. The kind of behavior that leads to recurring disciplinary problems at school usually indicates some sort of maladjustment. This frequently is caused by the interaction of the student with certain factors of his environment.

The Community. We read about the influence of the community on student conduct. Here we find a great deal of difference between rural and urban populations. The rural youngster relates to a community far less than does the urban student. Hence the influence of the community is reduced for rural youth.

The slum school and the behavioral problems encountered by its students have been widely discussed. One of the problems of school-age people in slums is that of leisure time. There is a strong tendency to spend this time on the streets, with little or no supervision. The frustrations that result from such nonproductive activity have their effect on conduct at school.

Another factor that is frequently associated with a slum community is the tendency of youngsters to overidentify with groups or gangs. Peer acceptance sometimes is based upon the degree to which the person will defy the law. Hence, the teacher may find himself dealing with conduct that is caused by motives based entirely in the community rather than in the school.

However, one cannot assume that community-based behavioral problems occur only in slum schools. Some youngsters build up attitudes of resentment or rebellion because of the overly regimented activities that are inflicted upon them by a middle or upper income community. Community pressures for conformity have subjected many children to an endless round of music lessons, dancing lessons, and other lessons of this nature. A few years ago some teen-age boys were arrested for stealing cars. They were from wealthy families, so money was not their motive. It developed that their conduct was essentially a protest against the type of community regimentation to which they were subjected.

There is always a question regarding what the teacher can do about such community-based problems. Obviously, he cannot remake the community. However, even though no direct action on his part may be feasible, it is important that the teacher know about such matters. Sometimes a kindly word of advice can help. Also, the teacher's information can be of real value to those people or agencies that are directly involved in trying to give assistance to students in this group.

The Home. The story is told of the first-grade teacher who said to a parent of one of her students, "If you won't believe what she says about me, I won't believe what she says about you." The home-school relationship is necessarily a very close one. School problems are carried home; home problems go to school. In fact, some of the more difficult behavioral problems with which teachers deal come from home. A few illustrations show this to be the case.

A third grader was usually a well-behaved, happy little girl. However, almost overnight her attitude changed completely. She became surly, rude, refused to do her work, and promoted quarrels on the playground. The teacher made discreet inquiries and learned that the child's parents were in the process of getting a divorce. While the teacher's scope of operations were limited, she was able to deal with the child in a more understanding way.

A teen-age boy was frequently sent to the principal's office for misconduct, especially during the first class period. He was never very communicative about his motives, but as the day wore on, he became more cooperative. The principal learned through a parent conference that there was a great deal of conflict between the boy and his father. Heated discussions between the two frequently occurred at breakfast. Hence, the boy was bringing to school certain resentments that derived from a home situation.

A third case was a girl who was both an academic and a behavioral problem. The family seemed to be very close, and the parents were greatly concerned over their daughter's difficulties. Over a period of time it developed that the girl simply resented the fact that both of her parents were career people, so that there was very little "family time."

This list could be continued almost indefinitely. However, the point is that in school we deal with people who come from homes—a wide diversity of homes. The conditions that prevail in these homes definitely influence the work that students do and the problems we have to handle. Hence it is essential that we know about the homes from which our students come.

The School. There is nothing natural about a school. It is purely a contrived situation, designed and supported by society. The school attempts to carry out certain functions assigned to it by that society. Hence, it is to be expected that some people will actively dislike such an institution.

What are some things about the modern school that might promote negative attitudes? There is regimentation. There is a mixture of failure with success. There are people. There are demands. There are rules. "The food in the lunchroom is terrible."

The point here is that some people simply do not like school. When they are required to attend, they are very likely to create problems of behavior. Many schools are trying to locate such students early, in the hope that they can be placed in special types of work which might more effectively meet their needs. However, a great deal remains to be done in this regard.

Preventing disciplinary problems

The best way to deal with a disciplinary problem is to prevent it. Yet some teachers of many years' experience still have difficulty in spotting potential trouble and eliminating it before it assumes major proportions. There are many steps teachers can take in this regard.

Plan Your Work. Many classroom behavioral problems grow out of sheer boredom. Consider, for example, the student who already knows the material—or the student who has no intention of learning it. Obviously the time spent in class by such students is simply time to be whiled away. What could be more likely to create a disciplinary problem? Yet if the teacher had developed a teaching plan that made provision for such students, problems could have been avoided. An essential part of planning is to be sure that everyone is constructively busy. It is as true now as it was when Benjamin Franklin said it, that "An idle mind is the devil's workshop."

Have Realistic Goals. The student to whom schoolwork means endless failure can create discipline problems. If he finds it impossible to gain recognition in constructive ways, he is likely to make his bid for recognition by creating problems.

It sometimes happens that a teacher dooms a student to failure simply because the teaching goals are completely beyond the student's capacity.

Not only should the goals be within reach of the student, they should be meaningful to him. The teacher who assigns to a student the task of copying a picture of a grasshopper out of a book might be setting up a task with an attainable goal. But what is its value? The student might simply refuse to do it because he sees no merit in the task.

Know the Students. The teacher who knows his students can usually predict responses. Yet many disciplinary problems arise because the teacher did not anticipate events as they actually happened. It is an integral part of planning for the teacher to look ahead in the matter of responses and to make provision to meet them.

Be Efficient. The average teacher unfortunately must devote considerable attention to housekeeping details. Consider, for example, the simple matter of calling the roll. After Johnny answers, nothing else is expected of him until the process is over. This gives rise to that dangerous situation of idle time. The teacher has to give attention to all sorts of details. Yet if he handles them efficiently and in a minimum of time, he will probably forestall problems.

Be Alert. When asked how she managed to get along with very few disciplinary problems among her students, a veteran teacher answered, "I out-think them." This may have been an oversimplification. However, this teacher very closely observed her class. As a result, she could spot potential trouble very early and could deal with it. For example, she noted that when two particular boys worked together in class, they tended to become somewhat rowdy. Without lectures or fanfare, she simply saw to it that these boys did not work together. A teacher at the upper elementary school level noted that two boys were "borrowing" bikes for unauthorized rides. He called the boys in, described the problem, and appointed them as a committee of two to "help put an end to this practice."

Behavioral problems seldom crop up suddenly. More commonly they result from a pattern of conduct over a period of time. If the teacher is alert and is conscious of little things, preventive measures usually are available.

A certain young man became a mathematics teacher. He

had a good background in his subject and was very interested in it. In fact, he was so interested that, while working at the blackboard, he would forget the class completely. He would work away, talking to the board, while the students went their own way. For obvious reasons, his period of service as a teacher was brief.

Be Friendly but Firm. Many students feel obligated to see what they can get away with in the matter of classroom conduct. Departures from the established standards cannot be ignored. Yet for the teacher to approach the task of correction with an attitude of embarrassment or apology is self-defeating. On the other hand, the use of ultimatums, threats, or temper tantrums is equally ineffective. If the teacher holds a private discussion with the student, pointing out in a firm but friendly way the standards of conduct that are to be observed, it usually helps. Incidentally, by making corrections out of class, the teacher is denying the student any form of group recognition that would accrue to him if the correction were made in class.

Handling disciplinary problems

You will note that the earlier section dealt with the prevention of disciplinary problems. Here we will take up some aspects of the work of the teacher in handling the problems that do occur.

Know the Policies. Many large school systems have established sets of policies governing the ways of coping with discipline. Some, for example, designate quite specifically the types of problems that should be handled by the teacher, the types that should be referred to the principal, and the types that should be passed along to higher administrative levels.

It is good to know in advance whether or not the school permits the use of corporal punishment by the teacher. Since practices in this regard vary widely among schools, it is never safe for the teacher to assume anything along this line. If there are prescribed conditions that must be met in the use of punishment, the teacher who proposes to use this treatment should be well informed about them.

Also, the teacher must know what constitutes an infraction of rules. Consider, for example, a new teacher who sent two high school students to the principal for smoking. In the school in which this teacher had previously worked, the boys would have been guilty of a major crime. However, under the rules of the new school, smoking was perfectly legal. Hence, the teacher's referral was a source of embarrassment to himself and to the principal.

In essence, the teacher should not deal with a disciplinary problem unless he is sure there *is* one. Then, before he proceeds, he should know the practices and policies governing such matters as they apply to the local situation. He should be sure that the action he takes is in keeping with such policies.

Be Clinical. What is the motive of the teacher in dealing with a misbehaving student? Is it to get even with him? Is it to win an argument? Is it to demonstrate to other students just how "tough" the teacher is? We cannot say that these and other such reasons have not entered into the situation occasionally. But you will recall that the word "discipline" grows out of the basic meaning "to learn." Hence, when we deal with a disciplinary case, our motive should be to teach the student a lesson—a lesson which he obviously needs.

There is always the danger that the teacher will become emotionally involved, that is, will yield to anger. This removes the teacher from the role of judge-teacher and places him in the role of prosecutor-executioner. If the teacher is to exercise calm judgment, he must display an adult approach to the situation. In short, he must keep calm.

There is another aspect of the clinical point of view that is important. The teacher needs to be diagnostic. Since behavior does not just happen, the teacher should strive earnestly to ascertain the root cause of the behavior problem. Frequently the cause is quite simple, such as a basic need for attention or recognition. However, many problems are far more complex.

While being clinical about the student, the teacher needs to apply some of the same methods to himself. Actually, there are cases in which the teacher promotes behavioral problems. Suppose that a fight occurs on the playground between two fourth-grade boys. It develops that the teacher who should have been supervising them was in the teachers' lounge at the time. Or suppose that a high school teacher has developed certain mannerisms that strike the students as being hilariously funny. Or suppose the teacher is simply short on temper and is inclined to "fly off the handle" at regular intervals. This list could be continued indefinitely. However, the important thing is that any time a teacher has to cope with a behavioral problem, he ought to engage in a bit of introspection to see if there is a lesson for him in the situation.

Make Referrals. In our efforts to educate "all the children of all the people," it is inevitable that we sometimes have students whose needs cannot be met by the classroom teacher. Some school systems employ specialists such as psychologists, social workers, and nurses. Others depend upon outside agencies to provide such services. However it may be handled, the teacher should know which referral services are available and the procedures to be used in making referrals. In behavioral cases which are too complex for the teacher, he should certainly feel free to make referrals to more specialized agencies.

QUESTIONS AND ACTIVITIES

1. What legal restrictions are placed upon the teachers of your community in the use of corporal punishment?
2. In retrospect, did you have any teachers who had difficulty in maintaining order? If so, what would you have done to improve the situation had you been the teacher?
3. Do you think "developing intelligent self-control" among students is too idealistic a goal? Why?
4. How would you evaluate suspensions and expulsions as disciplinary measures?
5. It is not unusual to hear a teacher refer to a particular student as a "born troublemaker." Do you think this is an adequate diagnosis? Explain.
6. What sociological changes are now under way in America that will proabably influence school discipline in the future?

Bush, Robert N., *The Teacher-Pupil Relationship*, Englewood Cliffs, N.J.:
Prentice-Hall, Inc., 1954.

Corsini, Raymond J., and D. D. Howard, *Critical Incidents in Teaching*,
Englewood Cliffs, N.J.: Prentice-Hall, Inc., 1964.

Josselyn, Irene M., *The Happy Child: A Psychoanalytical Guide to Emotional
and Social Growth*, New York: Random House, Inc., 1955.

Lee, Grace, ed., *Helping the Troubled School Child, Selected Readings in
School Social Work, 1935–1955*, New York: National Association of
Social Workers, 1959.

Prescott, Daniel A., *The Child in the Educative Process*, New York: Mc-
Graw-Hill Book Company, 1957.

Wallach, Michael A., and Nathan Kogan, *Modes of Thinking in Young
Children: A Study of Creativity-Intelligence Distinction*, New York: Holt,
Rinehart & Winston, Inc., 1965.

INDEX